NEW PIZZA

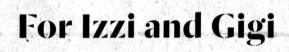

For Izzi and Gigi

STEFANO MANFREDI

NEW PIZZA

A whole new era for the world's favourite food

MURDOCH BOOKS
SYDNEY · LONDON

CONTENTS

New wave – new pizza   6

What is pizza?   8

Ingredients   14

Five great Italian pizzaioli   38

Pizza doughs   70

Pizza rossa   90

Pizza bianca   110

Roman pizza (precooked)   154

Roman pizza (predressed)   182

Filled, fried & sweet pizze   216

Index   238

New wave – new pizza

Pizza is probably the world's most popular fast food and wherever it has gone, it has taken on the characteristics of its new home. While Italy, and more precisely Naples, is where it all began, there's no doubt that pizza now belongs to the world. But something exciting is happening in pizza's spiritual home. What I call the 'new wave' of pizza has been gaining momentum in Italy in the last decade and that inspiring movement is the focus of this book.

I've been researching pizza in Italy for many years now and I've noticed a huge change in the way it is made at every step of the process. It has been led by chefs/pizzaioli whose curiosity and eye for quality has led them back to the fundamental building blocks of pizza-making, from the growing of the grain and the milling process to temperatures, fermentation and maturation times for the dough.

Where has this change in pizza-making led us? Much like the recent movement away from industrial white bread towards artisan loaves with natural leavening and specialist flours, it's a look back as well as a step forward. 'New wave' pizza-making is a movement that returns to pizza's origins before industrial flour milling, while at the same time using modern advances in stone milling, machinery and oven technologies.

This step forward in pizza-making has by necessity taken place outside Naples. If you look closely at pizza kitchens in Naples you'll find that many of them use highly refined '00' flour, as outlined by one of the groups set up to standardise Naples-style pizza. This flour is relatively cheap, has had the wheat bran and germ removed in the refining process and has the consistency of talcum powder. Now, there is nothing wrong with this and the use of '00' flour more or less defines the 'Naples-style' pizza as we know it today, but what happens when you use different flours, milled with stone and free of these strictures? What can be achieved when these flours are then used with different types of fermentation procedures? These are some of the questions we will look at in this book.

After all, even when pizza appeared in Naples in the first half of the eighteenth century, it would be over a century before the modern roller mill was invented. So, for at least a hundred years, stone-milled flour was used to make pizza. Granted, the bran was partly sifted out by pizzaioli even back then, but the grain was milled in its entirety, and this is fundamental to its structure. The roller mill brought us white flour. White flour meant uniformity, consistency and less technical ability needed on the part of the pizzaioli. As well, this flour lasts a long time and can therefore be exported and used to make a similar quality product around the world.

The other feature of 'new wave' pizza is the focus on quality ingredients to go on top. With the exponential spread of pizza post World War II and, more recently, globalisation, this fast food has become 'devalued'. In Italy, the margin on a typical pizza is so small that many of the pizzerie have developed a way to use cheap flour, short fermentation and maturation times, and poor ingredients to remain profitable. Now, not everyone adheres to these minimums, but with price pressures dictated by the market, the fact that stoneground flour costs more and that long, 'indirect' fermentation or a natural *lievito madre* (sourdough starter) take longer to make and are more involved, there is an incentive to take the easiest route. This approach is not just limited to Italy. As the pizza of Italy, and Naples in particular, is seen worldwide as a benchmark, the world for the most part follows.

This book will take the reader through what we do at my pizzeria, Pizzaperta Manfredi in Sydney, Australia. I have been a chef, running restaurants of the highest quality, for over 30 years. I have studied the methods and procedures of some of the protagonists of the 'new wave' pizza movement in Italy and this book is the result.

My hope is that the information here will guide home cooks and professionals alike to explore the possibilities of pizza-making and to take pizza back to what it once was – a healthy and delicious fast food.

STEFANO MANFREDI

What is pizza?

Pizza is a descendant of flatbread, the world's most ancient bread. Flatbread has been prepared since the time that people could grind grain, mix it with water and then cook it on hot stones, a griddle or in a makeshift oven. Whether it was made from corn, rice, potato, wheat, yam or another farinaceous edible plant, the flatbread sprang up in various parts of the world as people had the same basic idea. It was the first bread and it not only helped to hold other foods, but could be carried around and stored easily as a delicious snack or meal.

It appears that the version of pizza we know today – the round, puffy-bordered, wood-fired type – was born in Naples and was mostly confined to that city for over 200 years, as were the specialist pizzerie and pizzaioli who made pizza, along with the development of the special ovens that cooked it. In 1884, in her book *Il Ventre di Napoli*, Matilde Serao describes an attempt to open a pizzeria in Rome, just 200 kilometres (125 miles) to the north of Naples. It was a novelty for a while, but it ended badly, with the entrepreneur going broke. Sophisticated Rome looked down on this street food from the south.

The two centuries of isolation were essential for the refinement of pizza in Naples, which at the time was one of the most populous cities in Europe. Back then Naples was not the sprawling city it is today. It was confined to a much smaller area, becoming the most densely populated, as well as one of the poorest, cities on the continent. People lived in small rooms in buildings of up to seven storeys, a contrast to other European cities of the time whose buildings were, at most, half as high. Cooking was difficult and dangerous in these cramped conditions. A visit to the old part of the city today will attest to the narrow lanes and the density of the housing.

Pizza developed in these densely populated streets as a cheap fast food, sold by the slice from stalls set up right on the laneways where half a million people were crammed into an area a tenth the size of today's Naples. The refinement of this popular food was not only driven by the intensely competitive market of the city's streets, but also by the character of Neapolitans themselves. Antonio Mattozzi writes in his book *Inventing the Pizzeria – A History of Pizza Making in Naples*:

> Barrels of ink have been spilled describing the character of the Neapolitan. The marvellous natural setting, the fabulous blue sky, pleasing weather, and exceptional panoramas juxtaposed with the daily struggle for survival under difficult (albeit negotiable) conditions made the Neapolitan a cunning dreamer, romantic but pragmatic, kind and violent, but enormously creative. Imagination and creativity were lavished on the invention of new trades. One stood out for being so widespread: that of the pizzaiolo and the pizzeria.

In today's Naples there are associations that attempt to codify and protect the 'true' Neapolitan pizza, such as the Associazione Verace Pizza Napoletana (AVPN), although these associations are akin to political parties that can't seem to ever agree with each other. There may still be much debate, but the stringent list of defining characteristics is typified by those advanced here by one of the city's master pizzaioli, Enzo Coccia:

GEOGRAPHICAL LOCALISATION / The Neapolitan pizza was first made in the city of Naples by unknown people. According to Professor Mattozzi in his book *A Neapolitan History: Pizzerias and Pizzaioli from the Eighteenth through the Nineteenth Century*, as far back as 1807 there were 54 pizzerie in the city.

SELECTION OF FLOURS / The flour used for the production of the Neapolitan pizza is classified as 'type 00' according to Italian regulation (DPR 187/2001) with a W (flour strength index) value of 300/320.

PREPARATION OF THE DOUGH / The Neapolitan pizza dough is made through a direct method and the percentage of salt added to it doesn't exceed 3 per cent to 1 kg (2 lb 4 oz) of flour weight. The flour is incorporated *a pioggia* (like a gentle rain) and its maximum hydration value is between 57 and 60 per cent.

RISING TIMES / At 25–27°C (77–81°F) the Neapolitan pizza dough is left to prove for 12–16 hours.

LAMINATING OF DOUGHS / The Neapolitan pizza is shaped exclusively by hand.

GARNISHING / According to de Bourcard in his 1857 book *Habits and Traditions of Naples*, the Neapolitan pizza is historically seasoned with a set of ingredients found in the city of Naples.

OVEN / The Neapolitan pizza is baked in a semi-spherical wood-fired oven made of refractory bricks with a 120 cm (47 inch) diameter and 42 x 22 cm (16½ x 8½ inch) central mouth.

BAKING / The Neapolitan pizza is baked at a maximum temperature of 480°C (895°F) and the baking time should not exceed 50–60 seconds.

DIFFERENCES BETWEEN THE FINISHED PRODUCTS / The Neapolitan pizza is a round product with a variable diameter not exceeding 40 cm (16 inches), with characteristics of softness throughout its surface.

SERVICE / The Neapolitan pizza is usually entirely eaten by a single person.

One of the strengths of the Neapolitan pizza is that the style is unique and, because of these attempts to classify it, it's recognised and replicable around the world as a brand, even if this in itself is not an assurance of quality. One must never forget that the quality of a pizza is always dependent on the skill of the pizzaiolo and the ingredients used to make it. While trying to codify 'pizza', there is also a danger that the Neapolitans' innate creativity is being restrained and stymied and that their pizza may stop evolving.

Due to the strictures within its native city, pizza's evolution is, by necessity, now happening outside Naples. In Italy there has been in recent years a proliferation of pizzaioli who have been attracted to this popular, easily accessible and easily shared food that seemed ready for a quality makeover. After all, Italy alone serves am amazing 56 million pizze a week: almost one pizza per head of population.

Of course, even before the rise of the 'new wave' pizza movement, pizza had evolved to take in many styles and there are different interpretations of pizza everywhere in Italy. Apart from the original **pizza Napoletana**, there is **pizza a metro** (also called **pizza alla pala**) and, as the name suggests, this pizza can be a metre (40 inches) or more long. **Pizza all'Italiana** allows for transgressions outside the Naples style, while the Roman **pizza a taglio,** or **pizza in teglia,** is a rectangular pizza where the base is often precooked before toppings are added. **Pizza Siciliana** uses local Sicilian ingredients and, more and more, the rediscovered ancient wheat varieties of the island, especially the durum types. The new high-end **pizza a degustazione** (often called **gourmet**) is served one small slice at a time and often uses interesting flours and fermentation techniques, with a series of luxurious toppings. Add to these the **folded pizza (calzone)** and the **fried pizza,** and what we see is a typically diverse Italian take on a national obsession.

And to make it even more confusing, pizza can also mean **focaccia**, as I found out while travelling to photograph this book. In the town of Altamura, in Puglia, famous for its naturally leavened bread made from durum wheat flour, I came across a small bakery called Forno Antico Santa Chiara. The bread here is baked in a wood-fired oven dating back to the fourteenth century. The owner, Vito Macella, also makes focaccia at lunchtime after all the bread has been baked and the oven is cooling down. The dough for this is made with naturally leavened, locally grown and milled durum flour. The dough is shaped in a disc, a little larger than a standard pizza, and cooked directly on the stone floor of the oven. It is a little higher in the middle than a pizza, soft and moist, though chewy from the durum wheat. The result is what I would call pizza. Certainly not Naples-style, but every bit as delicious, as were the local cheese, vegetables and herbs used on top.

However, above all these considerations, the quality of a pizza must be defined by the quality of the flour, the method of fermentation and the maturation of the dough, the correct temperature, cooking time and oven used, as well as the quality of the ingredients that dress it.

In this book I will look at how the 'new wave' pizza movement in Italy has led to improved ways of forming pizza dough and a better understanding of the implications of using different types of flours, fermentation and maturation techniques and how these can all come together to create the highest quality pizza.

Vito Macella – Forno Antico Santa Chiara in Altamura.

THIS PAGE / The focacce at Forno Antico Santa Chiara made with local durum wheat flour. **OPPOSITE** / Vito Macella preparing his ancient oven.

Ingredients

I need to know the history of a food.
I need to know where it comes from.
I have to imagine the hands that have grown, worked
and cooked what I eat.

Carlo Petrini, Founder of the Slow Food Movement

In the more than 30 years that I've been in charge of restaurants, one of my most critical jobs has been to find the right ingredients. Perhaps it was the way I was brought up. My father always had a vegetable garden and a variety of fruit trees such as fig, apricot, peach, lemon and mulberry. He would bring sacks and boxes full of freshly picked fruits and vegetables to our restaurants. Even now, I'm obsessed with where ingredients come from and who grows, makes or fishes them. It should be no different with what goes into and onto a pizza.

It is fundamental for me to understand the ingredients I use in my restaurants by getting to know the territory and the people who produce them. And for me, visiting these producers as regularly as possible is crucial. For example, we use stoneground flours from Petra and Mulino Marino in Italy and some local flours from stone mills in Australia. I have visited both the Italian mills and I'm in the process of establishing relationships with the Australian mills. I've also visited our olive oil suppliers, Frantoio Franci in Montenero d'Orcia, Tuscany and Frantoio Cutrera in Chiaramonti Gulfi, Sicily.

Sometimes it's about finding one of the definitive producers of an ingredient in Italy so that I know what to look for in a locally made one. Australia has strict quarantine laws and prohibits the entry of a number of key ingredients, such as Italian salami, coppa and unpasteurised soft cheeses. I've therefore always travelled back to the source, the origin, to taste the ingredient as it has evolved in its own birthplace, its own territory, before choosing local ingredients.

For the dough

FLOURS

Flour is the starting point for making pizza. For too long it has been overlooked as a sort of given of our industrial age. As has been the case with so many of the foods we take for granted in this way, some of the more curious among us have reviewed how we produce what we eat and drink and, with a greater understanding, have tried to use technology to create something special.

There has been a revival of interest in artisan bread-making in the new world countries over the past decades. It runs along the same lines as wine, beer, salt and even sugar, whose producers have been looking carefully at what has been lost or removed in the industrial process that can contribute to flavour, texture, look, feel and general well-being for the consumer. Pizza is now having its turn and flour is where we have to start.

Flour can be made from many things, such as rice, corn, rye, buckwheat, lentils, beans, potato, chia, amaranth, teff, chestnut and so on. But it is flour milled from wheat that is most commonly used throughout the world, especially in bread and pizza, because it contains a large amount of gluten.

Gluten is a composite of the proteins gliadin and glutenin. These are present, along with starch, in the endosperm of wheat. Gliadin allows dough to be malleable and stretchy, while glutenin makes it tough and resilient. Gluten is also present in rye and barley flours, but in much smaller amounts. These two proteins make up around 80 per cent of the total protein in wheat berries and it is primarily the proteins in gluten that give wheat dough its wonderful elasticity and structure.

The wheat berry is made up of three basic parts once the husk (or hull) has been removed:

BRAN / The bran is the outside layer of the wheat berry and accounts for roughly 15 per cent of its weight. It is made up of soluble and insoluble dietary fibre, mineral salts and vitamins.

ENDOSPERM / This forms the largest part of the wheat berry, accounting for around 83 per cent of its total weight. It contains protein, sugar, carbohydrates, iron and soluble fibre.

GERM / The germ is the embryo of the wheat berry. It's the part that will germinate to form a new plant. It is the smallest part of the berry, making up 2 per cent of its weight. It is rich in oils and gives flour a 'nutty' flavour and perfume. It is also important because it contains complex B vitamins. In refined flours it is absent because these oils, or fats, inhibit very long storage times.

If you've made bread or pizza before, you will have noticed that when dough is worked properly it can be stretched thinly, almost like bubble gum. It's this ability to form an elastic structure within the dough that traps the carbon dioxide produced by fermentation. And it is these small carbon dioxide bubbles that make the dough rise. Once the dough is baked, these bubbles remain as holes (alveoli), giving the bread or pizza its texture. The size of the bubbles, the softness of the dough and the crispness or firmness of the crust can be controlled through a number of techniques, which will all be discussed later.

Wholemeal and whole-wheat flours

Also called **wholegrain** flour, **wholemeal** has been milled using the whole-wheat kernel. That is the bran, endosperm and germ.

To make **whole-wheat** flour the bran, endosperm and germ are separated and milled. The flour made with the endosperm then has proportions of bran and germ added back, depending on the sort of flour needed. With stoneground whole-wheat flour, varying portions of the outside bran layer can be removed before milling to give the desired results. It will have more or less colour depending on the amount of bran the flour contains.

The flours we use are **whole-wheat** (rather than wholemeal) and contain varying degrees of bran and the entire germ. Because they are stone-milled and not bleached, they are darker and a little coarser than other commercial flours. This will result in a pizza with a crust that's also a little darker, but more fragrant and tasty.

It's important that you find flours that work for you. This will mean research and perhaps contacting mills or flour companies for details. It's not that difficult. I've found milling companies on the whole are more than happy to communicate with clients who want to know more about their flours. It will also mean experimenting with different flours.

Modern industrial roller-milled white flours are made up almost entirely of the endosperm, removing both bran and germ. Their appearance is uniformly white. But industrial doesn't always mean 'bad'. It denotes a repetitious process with consistent results, nothing more, nothing less. There are many pizza-makers creating outstanding pizza with roller-milled flour. But there is a whole new world of pizza-making that can be explored with flours containing various degrees of bran and germ.

Flour classification

There's a great confusion about the way Italy classifies its flour. The majority of pizza dough recipes call for '00' flour and, given its prevalence in the Naples-style pizza, the home enthusiast and professional alike often believe this flour is 'the best'.

But what does '00' mean? And what of the other grades of flour? At the most basic level it's a classification of how fine or coarse a flour is milled, '00' being the finest and, in increasing coarseness, '0', '1', '2' and finally *integrale,* or wholemeal. With each grade there is a corresponding minimum percentage of protein allowed – the finer the grade, the lower the allowed minimum. Because it's a minimum allowed, it means in theory that across types of soft wheats, grown in different microclimates, it's possible for a '00' and '0' grade to have elevated protein contents, but it's much easier for the coarser grades because they contain more of the bran and germ, where extra protein can be recovered.

We tend to use types '1', '2' and 'intergrale' flours in our pizze and blend them when we need different results. These grades are naturally obtained in the stone-milling process.

In the roller-milling process, the germ and bran are removed and white 'plain' or '00' and '0' flour are made using the endosperm. The bran and germ are processed separately and added back to the white flour in various quantities. Because stone mills produce flour from the entire grain, it retains much of its protein content, rich in fibre and gluten, though there may, as mentioned earlier, be some of the outer bran layer removed prior to milling.

The other important measurement that we look for in flour is its 'working gluten strength' or W quotient. It's a numerical value that measures tenacity against extensibility of flour when mixed with water in dough. The higher the number, the more hydration (water) it can absorb and it can take a more complex and longer fermentation and maturation. This is a general W strength guide:

WEAK FLOURS / Up to W 170, these flours absorb around 50 per cent of their weight in water. These flours are used for biscuits, cakes and grissini.

MEDIUM FLOURS / From W 180 to W 260, these flours absorb up to 65 per cent of their weight in water. Used for direct fermentation doughs, olive oil-based breads and focacce.

STRONG FLOURS / From W 280 to W 370, these flours absorb up to 75 per cent of their weight in water. Used for indirect and natural fermentation doughs, sourdough breads and where long fermentation and maturation times are necessary.

There are also very strong flours with quotients of W 400 and these can absorb 100 per cent and more of their weight in water.

Note that if in your part of the world you cannot find stone-milled flours, then look for a 'bread' or 'high gluten' flour.

All flour is perishable and should not be kept for more than 3–4 months. Store in a sealed container or bag in a cool, dry place, preferably at around 18°C (64°F).

The wheat family

All the wheat species we have today belong to the genus *Triticum*. It is generally understood that the domestication of wheat species dates back to the Fertile Crescent (the ancient lands that ran along the Nile, Tigris and Euphrates rivers) around 10,000 years ago. The first domesticated wheat species were einkorn (*Triticum monococcum*) and emmer (*Triticum dicoccum*).

With domestication came thousands of years of selection by farmers and industry all over the world, which resulted in the species *Triticum aestivum*, our common 'soft' bread flour wheat, being the most planted type today.

Mention also needs to be made of spelt (*Triticum spelta*), which is used in a couple of recipes in this book. Together with einkorn and emmer, these three species are considered the grandparents of modern wheat. In Italy, depending on the area, the word 'farro' can mean any one of these three. The three species are similarly confused in other parts of the world, so when buying spelt, emmer or einkorn flour it is always advisable to look for the Latin names.

The second most cultivated wheat species is the 'hard' wheat *Triticum durum*, its cultivars used for dried pasta and bread, as well as certain types of pizze and focacce.

Another of the 'hard' species Khorasan (*Triticum turanicum*) and its sub-species Kamut are increasingly being used in pizza- and bread-making because of their high protein content and flavoursome results.

Rye (*Secale cereale*) is related to wheat and can be very useful in small percentages to give a dough a particular nuance in flavour. Rye flour is high in gliadin but low in glutenin and, because of this, it has a lower gluten content in comparison with wheat flours.

Once the basic dough recipes in this book have been mastered, you may like to play around by substituting some of these species in small percentages to see what can be achieved.

WATER

When water is mixed with flour the proteins contained in flour are activated and transformed into gluten, which gives the resulting dough its viscosity and elasticity.

The mesh that's formed through this action is dependent on the quality and quantity of proteins in the flour and this net traps the gases formed during fermentation. These trapped gasses are the reason the dough rises and bubbles.

The water used has to be of a certain quality for optimum results. It can't contain too many mineral salts as they inhibit leavening and chlorine can kill enzymes. To mitigate against this, we use a filter, which renders the water relatively free of these impurities.

Shop-bought bottled water can be used as a last resort. The water should be still, not sparkling, is best from glass bottles, and a check on the label will give the water's pH levels. Ideally, water should have a pH between 5 and 6. Testing kits can be bought online or in hardware or specialist shops. You should not use tap water as it contains chlorine.

YEAST

Yeast is made up of a group of single-celled organisms, primarily *Saccharomyces cerevisiae*, which belong to the fungi kingdom. Together with flour and water, the addition of yeast initiates the crucial fermentation phase of dough. Yeast feeds on sugars contained in flour, producing carbon dioxide and alcohol, which allow the dough to rise. There are two types that can be used:

COMMERCIAL YEAST / This comes in two types. Firstly as a 'fresh' compressed cake, which can be bought occasionally from specialist food stores. When I first began making pizza, this was what I used. It's highly inconsistent as it degrades with time.

Better to use is dried or instant powdered yeast, which activates when it comes in contact with water. The best results are obtained if the dried yeast is mixed with a small quantity of water before being added to the flour and more water to make the dough.

NATURAL YEAST / This is made by mixing flour and water and allowing bacteria from the air to ferment it. The resulting yeast contains *Saccharomyces* as well as lactic and acetic acids. It's commonly known as a 'sourdough starter' or, in Italian, *lievito madre* (mother yeast). Making pizza using your own yeast is very satisfying, though it does take some daily maintenance. The yeast needs to be fed regularly and kept at constant temperatures.

There are two distinct types of natural starters: a runny, liquid type and a solid type. The difference is primarily in the hydration or water content. In Italy, it's the solid type that is used more in pizza-making because it is easier to regulate hydration.

There are many methods for making a sourdough starter (see page 79). Those who wish to pursue this advanced method should do so and then substitute for dried or fresh yeast in the recipes at a ratio of 25 per cent sourdough for every kilogram of flour used.

There's no argument that natural yeast gives a different result to your pizza dough. But it takes time to prepare and time to maintain. Commercial yeast will give you more certainty and consistency across the whole year. Both types of yeasts have their place.

SALT

Salt not only brings out the flavour in dough — in much the same way as it seasons food — but also limits it from rising too quickly. If it rises too quickly, the yeast will expire before it has done its work.

Salt also acts as a preservative, stops the proliferation of unwanted bacteria and slows the formation of lactic acid. As well, it helps regulate the uniformity of the alveoli in the cooked dough.

When making dough it's important to always add the salt after mixing the yeast, water and flour. These last three need to react and bind. Adding salt in this phase will inhibit the process.

I use a natural sea salt for making my pizze.

EXTRA VIRGIN OLIVE OIL

Extra virgin olive oil is a fat but, unlike most other oils or fats, it has not been heated or chemically extracted. This means that it retains all its beneficial compounds and aromatic structure. Extra virgin olive oil acts to soften and flavour pizza dough but, like all other ingredients, it must be of good quality.

Extra virgin olive oil is used in dough to a maximum of 5 per cent of the weight of the flour. As well, extra virgin olive oil is used to drizzle onto the finished pizza.

THIS PAGE / Zio Eduardo harvesting his San Marzano tomatoes.

To dress your pizza

TOMATOES

Many who make their own pizze, make their own tomato passata. Some make it from ripe raw tomatoes, chopped and simmered slowly to cook out the water, with added ingredients such as onion, garlic and various herbs. But if you can find the perfect fresh tomato, all that's really necessary is to purée it, preferably by squeezing it by hand. You are looking for a pure tomato flavour to create the pizza base on which to build your other flavours, not the 'tomato sauce' you would normally put on pasta.

Many Italians make preserved whole tomatoes as a yearly family ritual, wherever they have migrated in the world. Some even grow their own tomatoes for both eating and preserving. Certainly, if tomato season brings you abundance, then preserving is both prudent and frugal, two qualities that form the basis of Italian cuisine. But the tomato smeared on a pizza dough base, preserved or fresh, has to have certain qualities. It must have a bright, consistently red colour. It must have few seeds and those it does have should be soft and barely perceptible. It should have a soft inner fibre and veins and its skin must be thin and easily peeled. And, above all, its flavour must be sweet with a balanced dose of acidity.

I tried a lot of different preserved tomatoes, both tinned and in glass, when I was looking for the right ones to use on our pizze: some squat, plum-like tomatoes from Sardinia, cherry tomatoes from Sicily, as well as many local Australian whole and mashed tomatoes. I settled, unequivocally, for a tinned whole peeled tomato from the volcanic soils around Mtount Vesuvius, near Naples.

Why use tomatoes preserved in tins or glass? The answer is simple: fresh tomatoes are at their very best for a very short time of the year, usually late summer and into early autumn. This is when their sugar content, colour and acid balance are at their optimum and preserving captures that moment. I can't imagine using hothouse-grown winter tomatoes that have been 'forced' to grow in artificial conditions. The flavour and texture are all wrong for a pizza.

The tinned tomatoes we settled on are San Marzano dell'Agro Sarnese-Nocerino DOP. It's a mouthful, but it's important to understand the classification. The DOP is a European certification that guarantees that what is in the tin is grown in the Sarno Valley. American writer and seed expert, Amy Goldman Fowler, author of *The Heirloom Tomato: From Garden to Table – Recipes, Portraits and History of the World's Most Beautiful Fruit,* has called the San Marzano, 'The most important industrial tomato of the twentieth century'.

Because San Marzano is a true (heirloom) variety, its seeds breed true from one generation to the next and this important tomato is now grown all over the world. But there is more to the quality of San Marzano than genetics. For nearly 300 years this tomato has been growing in the Sarno Valley. It is here where it achieves its optimum expression. Consequently, these tomatoes are in high demand, especially by the pizza market.

The DOP area is limited not only in size, but also in the quantity that can be produced from each hectare. Paolo Ruggiero, whose family runs Danicoop, a cooperative of San Marzano DOP farmers, estimates that the total production in a good year is 70 tons. That's just 70,000 kilograms for the entire world.

Let's just say that because of demand, there are constant scandals with misleading labelling, misrepresentation and outright falsifying of labels of San Marzano DOP. This is mostly a problem that occurs outside of Italy, where the European Union and Italian authorities have little chance of policing the markets. And often the product in question is much cheaper than the real thing.

The San Marzano DOP we use comes from Paolo Ruggiero's Danicoop. The cooperative has some fifty farmers ranging in ages from 60 to 80. Together with their families, they cultivate around 25 hectares within the DOP zone to produce the brand Gustarosso. It is part of the prestigious Presidio Slow Food, a collection of important artisan ingredients worthy of preserving. We also get a small quantity of their excellent Lucariello: a small yellow tomato with a delicate flavour.

THIS PAGE / San Marzano tomatoes are grown in the volcanic soil of the foothills beneath Mount Vesuvius. These wooden stakes attest to the laborious manual work carried out each year by the farmers. **OPPOSITE /** Zio Vincenzo and Zia Lina harvesting their San Marzano tomatoes.

Sarno is about 45 kilometres (30 miles) south of Naples, literally on the other side of Vesuvius and just a little inland from Pompeii. The fields are irrigated using the clean waters of the Sarno River. I visit them as often as I can. I've met some of the farmers and had lunch with them in the fields. I stay in touch with Paolo and our importer. We can be sure that what we are getting is the real thing. Each year we have to provide an estimate of the quantity we will commit to. That is set aside for us. Once we finish our allocation, there is no more until the following November, when the new harvest is processed and shipped.

By the time their tins of San Marzano DOP arrive in our pizzeria, they are twice the price of many other brands available in Australia, but I can be sure of what we are getting. We know where they've come from, who has grown and picked them, and that we are supporting an artisan farming community.

There are other excellent producers, such as Agrigenus, also a cooperative and also part of Presidio Slow Food. I have used their San Marzano and they are exceptional.

BUFFALO MOZZARELLA

Water buffalo were introduced into southern Italy as early as the seventh century, probably by the Arabs in Sicily and then by the Normans on the mainland. They adapted very quickly both to terrain and climate and were used as draught animals, although milk production gained in importance over time.

Today the water buffalo in Italy remain an important source of milk for making butter, ricotta and many diverse cheeses, such as caciocavallo, provola and, the most famous, buffalo mozzarella. This cheese is highly prized because buffalo milk is richer in fat and protein than dairy milk.

While buffalo milk mozzarella is made in many parts of Italy, and across the world, Mozzarella di Bufala Campana DOP is made in just two regions: Campania and Lazio, across the seven provinces of Caserta and Salerno and parts of Benevento, Naples, Frosinone,

ABOVE / Barlotti's classic mozzarella di bufala.

OPPOSITE / Near the town of Paestum there's an ancient Greek settlement, founded around 700BC, with a huge archaeological park nearby containing enormous Greek temples. The park is an important UNESCO World Heritage Site.

Latina and Rome. Along the coastal, southern end of Salerno province is the town of Paestum, which lies close to an ancient Greek settlement, and between this site and the Mediterranean coast is Barlotti, one of my preferred buffalo mozzarella producers. They have their own herd of water buffalo and make the most delicate mozzarella I've ever tasted.

Barlotti mozzarella is made with raw buffalo milk, in much the same way that fior di latte is made. The difference is that Barlotti doesn't put its mozzarella in a final salty water bath. This keeps the outer skin thin and delicate. The colour of the mozzarella is white porcelain and inside the skin it is made up of many thin, slightly elastic leaves formed from the initial repeated stretching. The internal colour is slightly darker than the outer skin and, when cut, it 'weeps' aromatic 'tears' that both taste and smell of sweet lactic ferments.

Once it has been made, the shelf life of this mozzarella is a short 4–10 days, depending on how it is stored. As it is made from raw milk, it has a shorter life than a pasteurised milk mozzarella, but the flavour and texture are superior.

FIOR DI LATTE MOZZARELLA

Fior di latte translates as 'flower of the milk'. This cheese originates in the Southern Apennines, though versions are made all through the Italian peninsula. It's a stretched curd cheese, made in a similar way to buffalo mozzarella, though using cow's milk. Some of the best is produced in the Lattari Mountains, above the Amalfi Coast, especially around the town of Agerola.

I visited the Fusco family in 2015 at their artisan facility, Fior d'Agerola. Here, raw cow's milk is obtained from several milkings over the course of a maximum of 16 hours. They don't use Jersey cows as they find the fat content of the milk too high and it gives the mozzarella a yellow colour with a taste that is too sweet. The preferred breed is the local Agerolese cow, whose milk produces a distinctly flavoured fior di latte.

After the milk comes in it is heated to around 38°C (100°F). Whey is added and mixed in, then rennet, and after 30–40 minutes the milk coagulates. The curd is broken up into small, hazelnut-sized pieces and allowed to ferment and mature for some hours. Once it

OPPOSITE / Fresh buffalo milk curd before it's placed in a hot water bath and stretched to form Barlotti mozzarella di bufala.
THIS PAGE / The curd is stretched continually in hot water until it is deemed ready to shape by the cheese-maker.

has matured it is ready for the *filatura*, the stretching of the curd. It is cut into pieces and placed in water at a temperature of 80–100°C (175–210°F). The curd is continually stretched and twisted by hand until the master cheese-maker decides it's ready. The curd is so elastic that it can be stretched to a thinness that resembles bubble gum.

It's now ready for the *mozzatura*: the shaping of the individual balls. From the word 'mozzare', which is where mozzarella gets its name, it means to squeeze a ball of stretched curd cheese from a piece and pinch it off. You can often see a join on an individual ball where this has been done. The balls can be made in a range of sizes, either by hand or machine. Finally, the balls are put in cold water to firm up and then into a salt brine solution.

BURRATA

This extraordinary fresh cheese is a member of the family of stretched curd cheeses that include mozzarella. It originates from the southern Italian region of Puglia – the heel of the boot.

Just north of Bari, the capital of the region of Puglia, is the town of Andria. It's on the coastal Murgia, a stretch of flat pastoral land stretching from north of Bari down to Brindisi, perfect for grazing sheep and cattle. In 2017 the burrata of this area was given its own denomination: Burrata di Andria IGP. It's here that Michele and Carmela Olanda, together with their family and dedicated staff, produce some of the best stretched curd cheeses in the world. In particular they are famous for their burrata.

For burrata, a sheet of fior di latte, about 5 mm (¼ inch) thick, is stretched to the required size to form a flat sheet in the shape of a circle, which can vary according to the size of the burrata. The shaping is expertly done, seemingly in the blink of an eye, using thumbs and fingers. It is then filled with mozzarella strings mixed with cream called stracciatella.

The thin mozzarella sheet is folded and tied at the top to form little 'moneybags'. The burrata are then dipped into a brine solution for

a few minutes to salt them. While Caseificio Olanda are known for their burrata and stracciatella, they also make excellent ricotta, caciocavallo and a fantastic cave-ripened caciocavallo di grotta. The food and wine magazine *Gambero Rosso* deemed their fior di latte one of the top ten in Italy.

ANCHOVIES AND COLATURA D'ALICI

One much-loved ingredient to dress a good pizza is the anchovy. Perhaps the most famous of all anchovies is that caught off the coast of the town of Cetara, on the Sorrentine Peninsula.

This picturesque town of a little more than 2000 inhabitants sits on a steep, amphitheatre-like hillside, looking down on its own beautiful harbour and beyond to the Mediterranean. It's here that for almost 70 years, Giulio Giordano's family have been salting and preserving the anchovies, or *alici*, that are caught by the fishermen of Cetara. Giulio explained that it's the deep water just off the coast and the perfect salinity that make the anchovies here so special.

He took us through the small front room, which serves as a shop and where various sizes of glass jars of neatly packed whole and filleted anchovies, sealed with the red and blue Nettuno label, sit on shelves. In the main room is a large table where men and women sit filleting anchovies and arranging them in the familiar large, wide-mouthed jars, all the while chatting. Further through still is a series of smaller alcoves with wooden barrels emitting a funky, though strangely attractive odour. It's here where the highly prized *colatura d'alici* is aged. This is Italy's fish sauce, made in the area since the thirteenth century when Cistercian monks modified the ancient Greek and Roman tradition of *garum*. This method salted and seasoned all manner of fish, including their innards, in the sun to make a paste and a liquid used to flavour various dishes.

Giulio explains the process. Freshly caught anchovies are gutted and their heads removed, all by hand. They are arranged in alternating layers with salt in a small wooden barrel called a *terzino*, from the word *terzo*, meaning 'a third', as the barrel is a third of the size of one of the local wine barrels. Once the layers reach the top, the

THIS PAGE / Barrels of salted anchovies in Nettuno's cellars in the town of Cetara, on the southern coast of the Sorrentine Peninsula. The famous colatura d'alici is formed over months and sometimes years. This 'fish sauce' dates back to the Romans.

THIS PAGE / Cetara's famous anchovy fillets. **OPPOSITE /** Hand-filleting anchovies at Nettuno.

THIS PAGE / At Santoro, in Puglia's Itria Valley, pork neck is seasoned with wild local herbs to produce Capocollo di Martina Franca.

barrel is closed with a wooden lid and a large stone is placed on top. The barrel is then labelled with the date and left for 12 months or more. When the liquid has 'ripened' it rises to the surface and the lid submerges due to its weight. A hole is made at the bottom of the barrel and a clear amber liquid begins to drip out. This liquid makes its way from the top, all the way through each of the layers, filtering sediment but picking up flavour and nutrients on the way.

This liquid is collected and bottled as colatura d'alici. On our visit, we saw some barrels were 4 or 5 years old. The colour of the liquid that came from these barrels was even deeper and darker and the flavour more intense and complex.

We've been using colatura d'alici in our restaurant dishes for some years now and, more recently, we've begun to use it judiciously as a final dressing on certain pizze with great success.

SALUMI

The great salumi of Italy are essential in our pizze and are used often as stars in their own right as well as supporting players. The various prosciutti, salami, pancetta and particular preparations like Calabrian 'nduja have a wide following and are relatively well known. They all make wonderful toppings for pizze.

However I want to concentrate on the lesser-known Capocollo di Martina Franca. One of the best producers is Santoro, situated in the small village of Cisternino in the Itria Valley.

The valley is home to the famous trulli, ancient-looking structures that are in fact relatively recent and were used essentially for tax evasion. Still they dot the landscape and add a lyrical quality to fields of wild fennel, red poppies, almonds and olives.

Santoro is the work of Giuseppe Santoro and Piero Caramia. Giuseppe is from Cisternino and Piero from Martina Franca. Together with their sons and daughters, they produce the famous Capocollo di Martina Franca as well as excellent salami, pancetta and cured pork loin.

The local pigs feed on acorns, roots and herbs from the nearby Macedonian oak forests, as well as the herbs, roots and shrubs of the surrounding hills. The capocollo comes as one piece taken from the upper part of the pig's neck. After careful trimming, it is dry-salted for 10 days. It is then washed and marinated with vin cotto, a reduction of the local Verdeca grape must. After 10 days it's put into natural gut, covered in a cotton sock and tied before a light smoking over oak bark, almond husks and wild local herbs. It is now ready to age in temperature- and humidity-controlled rooms for a minimum of 100 and a maximum of 180 days. The flavour is delicate and slightly fruity, with a pronounced nuttiness and an aroma of peppercorns, smoke and noble moulds.

Capocollo di Martina Franca should be thinly sliced just before adding to a pizza that's just come from the oven. The heat will enhance the flavour and perfume of the meat.

OLIVES

For me the default olive for pizza is the Gaeta. It comes from the coastal section east of Rome all the way down to the town of Gaeta. When it is brine cured, the skin is smooth and when it is salt cured, it's wrinkled. Either way, it's a meaty olive with a dark green to purple flesh and a flavour that's bitter, slightly sweet and briny like the sea.

Of course it's not the only olive that can be used, but it's the most versatile. Ligurian Taggiasche olives go extremely well with seafood. Fillets of the large green Bella di Cerignola olive are perfect when a mild olive flavour is required. This Puglian olive can also sometimes be black when allowed to fully ripen, giving it a more pronounced flavour.

It's always interesting to try different varieties of olives on pizza. The 'cracked' types tend to have more bitterness. Some of the Middle Eastern green olives with a slit in them can be sensational. Another 'cracked' type is the Sicilian Nocellara del Belìce, a khaki-green olive with flavours of artichoke and green tomato.

THIS PAGE / Santoro's Capocollo di Martina Franca, pancetta and salame maturing in temperature- and humidity-controlled rooms.

The darker the olive, the longer it has stayed on the tree to ripen. A warning though, many of the supermarket olives, especially the black ones, are picked green and then coloured with chemicals. It's always best to buy loose olives from a reputable providore and taste them first.

EXTRA VIRGIN OLIVE OIL

As well as being an essential ingredient in making my pizza dough and dressing the pizza once out of the oven, I prefer to cook everything in extra virgin olive oil. Sure, it's a little more expensive, but you can reuse extra virgin olive oil if you take care not to burn it and always strain it using a fine muslin cloth.

Don't believe those that say you shouldn't cook with extra virgin olive oil and, above all, that you should not deep-fry in it. Nothing could be further from the truth. Mediterranean cooks have known all along that extra virgin olive oil is not only wonderful to eat in its raw state, but is also the perfect cooking medium, even when deep-frying. But don't take my word for it. Let's have a look at the facts. The critical consideration when using any oil for cooking is its smoke point. This is the point at which oil begins to break down and form nasty substances that can be harmful and cause the food to taste rather unpleasant. Here is what The International Olive Oil Council says about deep-frying with extra virgin olive oil:

> When heated, olive oil is the most stable fat, which means it stands up well to high frying temperatures. Its high smoke point (410°F or 210°C) is well above the ideal temperature for frying food (356°F or 180°C). The digestibility of olive oil is not affected when it is heated, even when it is reused several times for frying.

Of course olive oil has always been a world apart from the other cooking oils. Firstly, it has always exquisitely expressed its *terroir*, that great French word that, when applied to wine, means the expression of its soil and particular microclimate. I'm not talking about blended olive oils here but about the traditional provincial pressing, the true expression of the land.

Olive oil is also different to other oils in its diversity and the expression of the land from which it comes. One never hears of a sesame oil coming from a certain region or a peanut oil exhibiting nuances and complexities. In fact, some seed oils such as grapeseed and sunflower are used by some cooks precisely because they are neutral and are merely the medium through which food is cooked. These are industrial products extracted using chemical solvents and heat, whereas extra virgin olive oil is simply extracted by pressing the juice of the olive and letting the water and oil separate naturally.

The idea of using a neutral oil is totally foreign to traditional Italian, and indeed Mediterranean, cooking. Imagine using an ingredient that adds absolutely nothing to the flavour or texture of a dish? The reason olive oil is used is because it tastes so good.

But theory is no substitute for practice and in Verona in April 1988, at Vinitaly, I witnessed a group of Italy's highly regarded producers of olive oil, for the benefit of the foreigners in attendance, deep-frying chips in extra virgin olive oil. They wanted to make the point that even the most severe cooking method, deep-frying, gave better results using extra virgin olive oil. The chips were spectacular.

Most Italians have grown up cooking with the first-pressed oil of the olive. Their mothers, grandmothers and great grandmothers used it. Mine did and it is one of the essential flavours that make Italian cooking genuine and authentic.

CAPERS

Capers are the unopened flowers of the *Capparis spinosa*, a Mediterranean bush that grows in particular hot dry climates, fed by salty sea air.

Caper bushes can vary in height up to 50 cm (20 inches). The bush has succulent, oval-shaped dark green leaves and beautiful pink and white flowers tinged with purple. It fruits like a berry, filled with black seeds. The bush flowers between late May and early September, which is when the closed flower buds are harvested.

These buds are picked before they blossom. They are green and firm and taste very strong. All picking is done by hand, the plants checked every few days as the season continues. It's a difficult task as the pickers have to bend down to check the low shrubs for the immature buds (the capers) in the intense heat of summer.

My preference is for capers in salt rather than in vinegar. When capers have been preserved in salt they retain their flavour and, most importantly, their texture. Kept in vinegar, capers become soft and taste predominantly of vinegar.

Ready capers by washing the salt off them first, and then soaking in a large bowl of fresh water. Leave for 15 minutes and then change the water. Repeat three more times, drain and then squeeze out the water from the capers. They are now ready to use.

I know that baby capers are very fashionable and for some pizze they work well. My favourite, however, are the larger ones. They have a lot of flavour and an almost crunchy texture.

Some of the best capers in the world come from the Aeolian Islands of Lipari and Salina, where they grow wild out of rocks and crevices. We use these as well as those from the island of Pantelleria. We also use tender young caper leaves that are cured and then preserved in extra virgin olive oil by Bonomo e Giglio (La Nicchia) on Pantelleria.

OREGANO

Dried oregano is a must for any pizzeria and is essential on that most simple of pizze, the Marinara. When you're dressing a pizza with only tomato, garlic, olive oil and dried oregano, it's important that the quality of each ingredient is the best you can find.

I've tasted dried oregano from all over the world, including many parts of the Mediterranean where it grows wild. Like all things, the flavour varies depending on where it grows.

The oregano we've settled on at Pizzaperta comes from the island of Pantelleria, situated in the Strait of Sicily, halfway between Marsala and Tunis. Bonomo e Giglio (La Nicchia), started in 1949 by Antonio Bonomo and Girolamo Giglio, produces some of the best dried oregano anywhere. It's richly fragrant and full flavoured, with none of the bitter notes that can occasionally be found in this dried herb.

FIVE
ITAL
PIZZ

GREAT

IAN'

IOLI

There are many pizzaioli I admire and who have influenced the way I look at pizza. To choose only five is like asking me to choose my five favourite songs or books. But this isn't a book about personalities or pizzerie. It's a book about the evolution of pizza-making and rediscovery of old methods in combination with new techniques. Rather than producing a list of the five 'best' pizzerie in Italy, I wanted to place this 'new pizza' into context and highlight a few protagonists that have changed, and continue to change, the world of pizza ... for me.

With each of them I have experienced moments that have caused me to stop and reassess my idea of pizza. It still happens and will no doubt continue to occur.

Enzo Coccia
Pizzaria La Notizia

'I'm not an artist. The musicians, sculptors, painters are. I am a craftsman in the service of one of the oldest activities of Naples, a pizzajuolo.'

With this statement we can understand where Enzo Coccia comes from. His craft is deeply rooted in the traditions, tastes and flavours of his territory. But it's his ability to experiment and use the highest quality ingredients in his restaurants that makes him stand out.

His first pizzeria, Pizzaria La Notizia 53, opened in 1994, was and still is a testament to his love of tradition and the perfect Neapolitan pizza. In 2010 he decided to challenge both himself and his often conservative customers and colleagues by opening at a second location up the road at Pizzaria La Notizia 94. Here he lets his imagination lead him; he experiments, has fun and, in turn, allows himself to break free of the tight noose of tradition. At La Notizia 94 you'll find uncommon pizze such as Baccalà in cassuola, a combination of San Marzano tomatoes, black Gaeta olives and pearl-white cubes of salted cod finished with parsley and basil.

When last I visited he was deep in conversation with some of his floor staff working on the presentation of a new panino. Soon we too were pulled into the intense world of Enzo Coccia, where every element that concerns food is considered of utmost importance.

What fascinates me about Coccia is his ability to reach back into history and reinterpret and rework ancient traditions to come up with something new and fresh. At Pizzaria La Notizia 94, his Citreum pizza is a nod to Roman traditions and uses the sweet zest of the famous lemons from the island of Procida, just off the Naples coast. The grated zest is used as a foil on a unique pizza of buffalo mozzarella and air-dried buffalo fillet, a sort of buffalo bresaola.

Enzo has helped me understand the beauty of pizza in Naples. The style is unique and its greatness lies in its simplicity, the character of its people and the quality of Campania's great produce.

Pizzaria La Notizia, 53
Via Caravaggio 53, Naples

Pizzaria La Notizia, 94
Via Caravaggio 94, Naples

www.pizzarialanotizia.com

THIS PAGE / Enzo Coccia's pizza is ready. **OPPOSITE** / Just a few of the best ingredients are added.

Enzo Coccia's Pizza alla procidana (Roast tomatoes, smoked scamorza, garlic and herbs)

Served at the Pizzaria La Notizia 94, Pizza alla procidana has the same colours as the classic Margherita, but is modelled after an eighteenth century recipe. If the Margherita is the queen of pizza, Coccia calls the Pizza alla procidana the king.

INGREDIENTS

250 g (9 oz) ball of basic pizza dough
  (see pages 74–77), shaped
  (see pages 80–83)

60 g (2 oz) smoked scamorza cheese,
  thickly grated
10 fresh basil leaves
2 tablespoons extra virgin olive oil

ROAST TOMATOES
8 ripe medium tomatoes, roma (plum)
  or egg-shaped
2 teaspoons extra virgin olive oil
¼ teaspoon sea salt

GARLIC AND FRESH HERB MIX
2–3 garlic cloves
25 g (1 oz/½ cup) fresh basil
10 g (¼ oz/½ cup) fresh parsley
15 g (½ oz/½ cup) fresh oregano
¼ teaspoon sea salt

METHOD

FOR THE ROAST TOMATOES / Preheat the oven to 180°C (350°F). Cut each tomato in half and place on a baking tray. Sprinkle with the olive oil. Season with a couple of pinches of salt and roast for 12–15 minutes or until the tomatoes have softened and are tender without having split. Remove and set aside to cool.

FOR THE GARLIC AND FRESH HERB MIX / Place the garlic, herbs and salt on a chopping board and chop until fine. Place in a bowl until needed. Though you'll want to make more than one pizza, any left-over mix can be stored in the refrigerator for up to 3 days.

TO ASSEMBLE / Place a large tile in your oven for the pizza, then preheat to full heat (without using any fan-forced function) for at least 20 minutes (see page 89). Scatter the roast tomatoes on top of the shaped pizza base, leaving the edges clear to about 3–4 cm (1½ inches). Add the grated scamorza and finally the basil leaves. Sprinkle a tablespoon of olive oil over the lot and place the pizza in the oven for 3–5 minutes until cooked, turning to get an even colour. Remove once cooked and scatter with 2 teaspoons of the garlic and herb mix. Finish with the final tablespoon of olive oil.

Makes one 30 cm (12 inch) pizza

Patrick Ricci

Terra, Grani, Esplorazioni

Patrick Ricci is one of a kind. A true creative in the (mostly) conservative world of pizza, his approach is poetic, lyrical and often romantic. He has the disposition of the 'outsider' and manages to communicate this complex amalgam through his ferments, dough and pizze.

A few short years ago Patrick travelled the world working for the Italian design firm Pininfarina as a quality manager. He describes his 'aha' pizza moment as (my translation):

> Like being locked in a room, seeing the same things over and over, a sad, boring and, above all, mental darkness. Then one day you open a door and find yourself in front of the blueness of the sky, infinite light and air. What's left behind is spent, old and stale. You don't want to return but keep walking forward and explore the infinite that's ahead.

His Capitanata pizza (see page 52) is a case in point. He calls it 'A memory of a voyage in Puglia'. He told me it started with the sweet, flat Zapponeta onion, grown in the sandy coastal soils of northern Puglia. From there he built the pizza with other iconic products of the region.

Ricci's menu is dotted with similarly evocative titles, such as Piogge d'Aprile or 'April showers', with snails, black truffle, garlic-scented olive oil and a bright green swirl of parsley salsa. La Nonna is his remembrance of when he was little and recalls his grandmother's bruschetta made with extra virgin olive oil, oregano and the deeply flavoured small tomatoes from the volcanic soils of Vesuvius (Pomodorini del Vesuvio DOP).

But while Ricci's toppings are unique, the quality, texture and flavour of his bases are exceptional. He produces two types of doughs, one using wheat and the other using spelt. Both are stoneground, germ included. They are different to the Naples style and closer to the crisp crust occasionally seen with a Roman-style pizza. He matches them to the toppings as he sees fit.

His restaurant is in the picturesque town of San Mauro Torinese, just outside Turin. I make it a point to go there each time I'm in Italy and have got to know Patrick and his partner Patricia Rea better with each visit. We have become friends.

To see where pizza outside Naples is headed, this is one of the places that is pushing the boundaries. Here, Patrick will challenge you and Patricia will make you feel comfortable, as if you were at home.

Patrick Ricci – Terra, Grani, Esplorazioni
Via Martiri della Libertà, 103 – San Mauro Torinese (To)

www.pomodoroebasilico.org

OPPOSITE / These centuries-old Puglian trees still produce olives. **THIS PAGE** / Structures called *trulli* are a feature of the landscape of central Puglia.

Patrick Ricci's Capitanata: Ricordo di un viaggio in Puglia (A memory of a voyage in Puglia)

Patrick Ricci's creations are lyrical as well as delicious. As he says, 'Pizza is emotion, feelings, sensuality, colour, gastronomic play, infinite exploration. It's courting and study, knowledge, curiosity and endless trial and error.'

INGREDIENTS

250 g (9 oz) ball of basic pizza dough
    (see pages 74–77), shaped
    (see pages 80–83)

Sea salt
100 g (3½ oz) burrata
1 red chilli, cut into thin rounds
6–8 sprigs of fresh basil leaves
1 tablespoon extra virgin olive oil

YELLOW TOMATO PASSATA

3 kg (6 lb 12 oz) yellow tomatoes
½ teaspoon sea salt
1 teaspoon extra virgin olive oil

SLOW-COOKED ONION

3 tablespoons extra virgin olive oil
3 kg (6 lb 12 oz) sweet white onions,
    thinly sliced
½ teaspoon sea salt
200 ml (7 fl oz) vegetable stock

METHOD

FOR YELLOW TOMATO PASSATA / Cut each tomato in half and, using a teaspoon, remove the seeds. Place the tomato halves with the salt and oil in an ample saucepan and heat for about 15 minutes over a medium–low flame with the lid on until softened, stirring every few minutes. Place in a mouli (food mill) and process so the tomato pulp passes through and the skins are left behind. Extra passata will keep for up to 6 days in the fridge.

FOR THE SLOW-COOKED ONION / Heat the olive oil in a large frying pan and add the onion and salt. Reduce the heat to medium–low and simmer, occasionally stirring, for about 20–30 minutes until the onion is very soft but not coloured. Add the stock and keep simmering gently until the pan is dry and the onion golden – about 30 minutes or more depending on the heat. Extra onion will keep for up to a week in the fridge. Bring to room temperature before use.

TO ASSEMBLE / Place a large tile in your oven for the pizza, then preheat to full heat (without using any fan-forced function) for at least 20 minutes (see page 89). Spread 4 tablespoons of the passata onto the shaped pizza, leaving the edges clear to about 2 cm (¾ inch). Scatter 4 tablespoons of the onion on top and then season with a couple of pinches of salt. Place the pizza in the oven for 3–5 minutes until cooked, turning to get an even colour. Remove and spoon dollops of burrata on top. Place one or two chilli slices on each burrata dollop and finish with a sprig of basil leaves. Drizzle with the olive oil.

Makes one 30 cm (12 inch) pizza

Simone Padoan
I Tigli

When we talk of 'new pizza' in Italy, the name that comes immediately to mind is Simone Padoan. He was one of the first, if not the first, to bring the chef's critical eye to the process of not only making pizza, but also presenting it.

Padoan opened his restaurant, I Tigli, at San Bonifacio in 1994, but his passion for restaurants and pizza began much earlier when he decided to change how he approached not only the way he made pizza, but also how it was presented.

I remember going to I Tigli for the first time. The experience was akin to fine dining, with all the accoutrements of beautiful linen, stemware and china and service to match. Indeed, his mission has always been to fuse pizza with high cuisine.

The wine list at I Tigli is extensive and thoughtful with a fitting selection of Italy's modern 'skin contact' and 'natural' wines, such as Gravner, Camillo Donati, Emidio Pepe and Occhipinti, as well as an international selection.

But the revolution is on the plate. While pizza was born as a simple, everyday street food made with flour, yeast and water, Padoan's pizza is anything but simple. He uses special flours that are stone-milled, and fermentation and maturation times are extended.

His pizze are cooked in a wood-fired oven, but at much lower temperatures than the Naples style. Typically, his are cooked at a maximum of 300°C (570°F), while Neapolitan pizza cooks at around 450°C (840°F). This affects the cooking times as well. Padoan's thicker pizze need more time to cook and stay in the oven for 4–5 minutes, while those of Naples generally cook in 60–80 seconds.

The other differences are the low cornice and the high, developed centre of the cooked base. These allow the pizza to hold more substantial toppings and mean Padoan can play with greater freedom, creating a pizza degustazione (gourmet pizza) with ascending flavours, from delicate to more assertive and bold.

I Tigli
Via Camporosolo, 11 San Bonifacio (Verona)

www.pizzeriaitigli.it

Simone Padoan's Pere ubriache, caprino alla cenere (Drunken pears, ash-rind goat's cheese)

The Tarocco is a variety of blood orange and is the most popular orange in Italy, loved for its sweetness and lack of seeds. Padoan also uses erica honey to finish this pizza. The honey is produced from Erica arborea, *a small bush native to southern Europe with pine needle-like leaves and small, white, bell-shaped flowers.*

INGREDIENTS

250 g (9 oz) ball of basic pizza dough
    (see pages 74–77), shaped
    (see pages 80–83)

1 Kaiser pear (also called Beurré Bosc)
120 ml (4 fl oz/½ cup) sweet white wine
½ teaspoon sugar
1 blood orange (Tarocco)
90 g (3½ oz) fior di latte mozzarella,
    cut into 1 cm (½ inch) cubes
A pinch of sea salt
A small handful of rocket (arugula),
    chopped
80 g (3 oz) ash-rind goat's cheese log,
    sliced into 8 rounds
8 pecan halves, shelled
2 teaspoons erica honey (or other
    dark variety)

METHOD

TO ASSEMBLE / Peel the pear and place in a sous vide bag (see note below) with the wine and sugar and seal. Place the bag in a water bath, heated to 63°C (195°F), and leave for 20 minutes. Remove the pear, cut in half, take out the core and slice into eight pieces from top to bottom. Wash the orange and dry it, then cut into 3 mm (⅛ inch) slices, including the skin. Place the slices on a cake rack and dehydrate in the oven at 90°C (195°F) for 70–90 minutes. The slices should be dry, but still a little soft. Cut each in half to form semicircles.

Place a large tile in your oven for the pizza, then preheat to 250°C (500°F) (without using any fan-forced function) for at least 20 minutes (see page 89). Place the pear slices, points to the centre, on the pizza base like eight spokes of a wheel. Scatter the base with the mozzarella cubes and a pinch of salt. Place the pizza in the oven for 4–6 minutes until cooked, turning to get an even colour. Once out of the oven, cut the pizza into eight wedges. On each wedge place some rocket, a half slice of dehydrated orange, a slice of goat's cheese and a pecan on top. Finish with a drizzle of the honey on each piece of cheese.

Makes one 30 cm (12 inch) pizza

NOTE / More than one pear can be done here and the pears can be kept refrigerated for up to 2 weeks. For four pears, double the wine and sugar. If you don't have a sous vide, use a snap-lock plastic bag (remove all the air before sealing) and bring a pot of water to the correct temperature using a thermometer as a gauge. Maintain this temperature by adjusting the heat source. It's not ideal, but does work if carefully monitored. The use of a simmer mat between the heat source and pot helps keep the temperature even.

Gabriele Bonci

Pizzarium

Much has been written about Gabriele Bonci and his 'hole in the wall' Pizzarium in Rome, not far from the Vatican. For those who enjoy sampling the very best pizza, Pizzarium is perhaps worthy of a similar pilgrimage as that taken to St Peter's, to taste the creations of this master of Roman pizza.

Pizzarium really is a 'hole in the wall' on a nondescript side street with a plain brick frontage and a large name sign over the door in a neo-sixties wavy font. Above, in smaller letters and contained in ovals resembling skateboards, are two more pieces of information: 'Pizza a Taglio' and 'Rosticceria'. Inside there is barely room to order, let alone sit down. I'd imagine the entire shop to be only around 30–35 square metres. Eating here is a stand-up affair.

Welcome to that great Italian pizza tradition – Roman pizza a taglio, which translates as 'pizza by the slice'. This is not the round, Naples-style pizza, cooked for a brief minute or so in volcanic temperatures. Instead, the dough is laid out in an oiled tray, a *teglia*, and cooked at domestic temperatures for 10–25 minutes.

Once cooked, the base can be finished with the necessary toppings. On entering Pizzarium, you will find a window showing a kaleidoscope of pizze. You choose the ones you want, the quantity, and the pieces are cut with scissors, weighed and heated in a small deck oven before being wrapped for you, ready to eat.

For me, Bonci has achieved something special with Pizzarium. He has taken what is essentially an Italian fast food and lifted it to a quality as high as any fine restaurant food anywhere. He has achieved this in a way that is extraordinarily clever, by maintaining pizza's identity as an everyday food, yet at the same time revolutionising all the steps, one at a time. His attention is focused on everything from the flours (he experiments with many old varieties and collaborates with mills) to the fermentation methods and cooking times and from each particular producer to the quality of the ingredients that top the pizze. Bonci has a particular affinity with vegetables. Some of my favourites of his pizze are those with boiled potatoes cooked on top of the dough. But all his creations use vegetables as a protagonist as well as in supporting roles.

There is also another side to Bonci that needs to be mentioned. His ability to communicate across all modern mediums means that he is respected and influential in various markets. Not only is he a regular on mainstream Italian television, but also in newspapers, magazines and books. He is prolific on Facebook and his posts are always interesting and 'on message'.

Pizzarium, Via Della Meloria, 43, Rome

Mercato Centrale di Roma, Via Giolitti, 36, Rome

www.bonci.it

THIS PAGE / Ordering at the counter at Pizzarium. **OPPOSITE** / Gabriele Bonci's pizza creations are Italian street food of the highest quality.

Gabriele Bonci's Pizza ricotta, cachi e 'nduja
(Roman pizza with ricotta, persimmons and 'nduja)

Bonci uses sheep's milk ricotta for this. If it is not available, cow or buffalo milk ricotta is suitable.

INGREDIENTS

1 sheet of Roman-style pizza dough
   (see pages 84–88), precooked
   (see page 89)

500 g (1 lb 2 oz) sheep's milk ricotta
   cheese
400 g (14 oz) 'nduja
6 very ripe persimmons, halved (see note)
Sea salt
200 g (7 oz) hazelnuts, roasted and
   skinned, coarsely chopped
3 tablespoons extra virgin olive oil

METHOD

TO ASSEMBLE / Place the pizza sheet on a serving plate as a large piece or cut, using scissors, into individual tiles. Spoon some dollops of ricotta here and there on top. Using a teaspoon, place some 'nduja on each dollop of ricotta and then a spoonful of persimmon flesh. Season with a little salt and sprinkle with the chopped hazelnuts. Finish with the olive oil.

Serves 6–8

NOTE / There are two distinct types of persimmons, with many varieties in each type. The first is the astringent type. When firm it has a bitter astringency that makes the mouth pucker. This type of persimmon needs to get very soft and jammy, the skin barely holding the flesh inside, before eating. As the fruit ripens, the tannins subside and eventually disappear, the astringency turning to sweetness. This is the variety used for this pizza. The other type of persimmon, the non-astringent type, can be eaten firm and crisp like an apple.

THIS PAGE / The display window at Pizzarium.

Antonio Pappalardo
La Cascina dei Sapori

Perhaps the most influential person in my pizza education has been Antonio. He came into my restaurant when he and his wife, Alessandra, were on their honeymoon in Sydney. We chatted, exchanged details, and I promised I'd go to their restaurant next time I was in Italy.

That was some years ago and since then our friendship has grown. We have travelled through Italy together in search of great pizza and great produce, looking for the characters and artisans who toil to achieve excellence so that we can present to our guests the best of Italy – *la bella Italia*.

Pappalardo was instrumental in the training and setting up of my pizzeria Pizzaperta. He spent a month with my pizzaioli pre-opening, showing them how to work with flours other than the usual highly refined '00' flour. We began using stoneground, whole-wheat Petra flours from Molino Quaglia, based in Padova, and had them imported for the first time to Australia. While we are now beginning to explore other flours, local and imported, and other techniques to give us our own identity, it was Antonio who showed us the foundations from which we are now evolving.

Antonio is from Naples, but his family moved to Brescia when he was small. They had a restaurant and, as he says, the restaurant chose him. After working in a restaurant, bakery and a pizzeria, it was the latter that sparked his interest. Perhaps all Neapolitans have pizza in their blood, but Antonio wanted more and set out to discover where pizza could take him and where he could take pizza.

He can experiment because he is no longer in Naples and has a loyal and growing clientele in the greater Brescia area that love nothing more than going to his restaurant, La Cascina dei Sapori, and trying his latest creations. He changes the menu with the seasons. There may be a pizza with tataki of tuna, ricotta and toasted linseed or one with *gambero rosso* (red prawns/shrimp), grilled fennel and burrata. There has even been a pizza called Ricordo d'Australia (memories of Australia) with macadamia cream, grilled scallops, prosciutto chips and macadamia crumble.

Antonio's team feels like a family. His mother provides many traditional preparations that ground his cuisine in classic home cooking, while a dedicated brigade prepares some of the best and most innovative pizza in Italy.

La Cascina dei Sapori
via Almici, 1 - Rezzato (Brescia)

www.lacascinadeisapori.it

Antonio Pappalardo's 'Nduja, fior di latte, friggitelli e caprino della val sabbia ('Nduja, fior di latte mozzarella, long chillies and goat's cheese)

This pizza is a journey from Italy's south to north that mirrors Antonio's own. The fior di latte mozzarella is made in Agerola, close to where Antonio was born, and 'nduja is the hot spreadable salame from Calabria. The friggitelli are preserved sweet green capsicums (peppers) popular especially in the north of Italy and often available pickled in jars in speciality shops. Finally, the caprino is a goat's milk cheese from the Sabbia Valley, northeast of Brescia. Another firm goat's milk cheese can be substituted, though it will have a different flavour.

INGREDIENTS

250 g (9 oz) ball of basic pizza dough
(see pages 74–77), shaped
(see pages 80–83)

100 g (3½ oz) fior di latte mozzarella,
thinly sliced
8–10 friggitelli
8 teaspoons 'nduja
2 tablespoons caprino della val sabbia,
coarsely grated
1 tablespoon extra virgin olive oil

METHOD

TO ASSEMBLE / Place a large tile in your oven for the pizza, then preheat to full heat (without using any fan-forced function) for at least 20 minutes (see page 89). Spread the mozzarella slices onto the pizza base, leaving the edges clear to about 2 cm (¾ inch). Scatter the friggitelli on top and then dollop the 'nduja here and there. Place the pizza in the oven for 3–5 minutes until cooked, turning to get an even colour. Once ready, remove from the oven and sprinkle with the grated goat's cheese. Drizzle with the olive oil.

Makes one 30 cm (12 inch) pizza

PIZ
DOU

ZA
GHS

In this section I set out the methods for making pizza doughs. Firstly there are the round, Naples-style pizza doughs and then the Roman-style doughs, cooked in a rectangular tray. There is also a recipe for lievito madre, or sourdough starter, which can be used instead of commercial yeast. It's a lot more work, but an advanced method to try.

You'll notice that there is no use of the Neapolitan-preferred 'oo' flour here. 'New pizza' is about exploring ingredients and the most fundamental is the grain that makes up the flour. Some pizzaioli go to great lengths in this regard, sourcing their own wheat and having it milled to their specifications. Yes, it's obsessive and geeky, but no more obsessive than growing your own produce if you have a restaurant.

The recipes here begin with simple procedures and, when you feel confident, you can move on to the more complex. It's a matter of finding the method that works for you.

Basic pizza dough
Direct method

The direct method for producing pizza dough is the easiest because all the ingredients are mixed together at about the same time. This is the method that the large majority of pizza-makers use because it's simple and quick.

For our recipes, however, we extend the maturation phase of the dough in the refrigerator so the final cooked pizza is easily digested and the flavour of the wheat maximised. Using an unrefined, stoneground whole-wheat (not wholemeal) flour is important because of its rich nutrients and the fact that it means less yeast is needed for fermentation and the maturation phase is thus more effective.

Fresh yeast dough

This recipe is for making pizza at home using 'fresh' or compressed yeast. Each 250 g (9 oz) ball of dough will make one 30 cm (12 inch) pizza, which feeds one person.

INGREDIENTS

1 kg (2 lb 4 oz/6⅔ cups) unbleached, stoneground
     whole-wheat flour or strong bread flour
550 ml (19 fl oz) water at room temperature
8 g (¼ oz) fresh (compressed) yeast
20 g (¾ oz) sea salt
30 ml (1 fl oz) extra virgin olive oil

METHOD

Place the flour and 500 ml (17 fl oz/2 cups) of the water in a mixer fitted with a dough hook attachment. Begin mixing on a low speed and keep mixing until the flour has absorbed all the water but is still not smooth. This should take only 3–4 minutes. Stop the mixer and let the dough rest in the bowl for 15–20 minutes.

Meanwhile, dissolve the yeast in the remaining water. Once the dough has rested, turn the mixer on to medium and add the dissolved yeast. Two minutes later, add the salt, mix for 2 minutes and then add the olive oil. Keep mixing until the dough is shiny and homogenous, about 6 minutes. Turn the speed up a little and mix for 2 minutes more.

A good way to check the elasticity is right is to stretch a piece of dough and if it forms a strong, transparent membrane without breaking (similar to blowing a bubble with gum), it is ready. Let the dough sit, covered with plastic wrap, for 30 minutes in winter or 15 minutes in summer. The dough is now ready to be shaped into balls and then rested further in the refrigerator before shaping into discs (see pages 80–83).

Makes 6 pizze (250 g/9 oz each)

Dried yeast dough

This pizza dough is made using easily available dried (powdered) yeast, which gives very consistent results. Each 250 g (9 oz) ball of dough will make one 30 cm (12 inch) pizza.

INGREDIENTS

1 kg (2 lb 4 oz/6⅔ cups) unbleached, stoneground
     whole-wheat flour or strong bread flour
550 ml (19 fl oz) water at room temperature
2 g (¹⁄₁₆ oz) dried (powdered) yeast
20 g (¾ oz) sea salt
30 ml (1 fl oz) extra virgin olive oil

METHOD

Place the flour and 500 ml (17 fl oz/2 cups) of the water in a mixer fitted with a dough hook attachment. Begin mixing on a low speed and keep mixing until the flour has absorbed all the water but is still not smooth. This should take only 3–4 minutes. Stop the mixer and let the dough rest in the bowl for 15–20 minutes.

Meanwhile, dissolve the yeast in the remaining water. Once the dough has rested, turn the mixer on to medium and add the dissolved yeast. Two minutes later, add the salt, mix for 2 minutes and then add the olive oil. Keep mixing until the dough is shiny and homogenous, about 6 minutes. Turn the speed up a little and mix for 2 minutes more.

A good way to check the elasticity is right is to stretch a piece of dough and if it forms a strong, transparent membrane without breaking (similar to blowing a bubble with gum), it is ready. Let the dough sit, covered with plastic wrap, for 30 minutes in winter or 15 minutes in summer. The dough is now ready to be shaped into balls and then rested further in the refrigerator before shaping into discs (see pages 80–83).

Makes 6 pizze (250 g/9 oz each)

Basic pizza dough Indirect method

The indirect method uses two (or more) phases for producing the dough. More time and labour are involved, but the results are great in terms of flavour, texture and digestibility. Ambient, or room, temperature affects the living dough. If it is cold, the dough takes time to develop and if it's warm, it moves quickly. Resting dough outside the refrigerator requires judgment, experience and practice. In this recipe the first dough must be kept at 16–20°C (60–68°F), which may be tricky during warmer parts of the year. At Pizzaperta, we have a purpose-built cabinet that sits at around 16°C (60°F). If you have a wine cabinet, they are also excellent. Otherwise, a cellar or insulated room in the house can be used. I've even successfully improvised a portable cool box with a couple of large ice cooler bricks.

FOR THE FIRST DOUGH (BIGA)

1 kg (2 lb 4 oz/6⅔ cups) unbleached, stoneground
    whole-wheat flour or strong bread flour
450 ml (16 fl oz) water at room temperature
6 g (⅛ oz) dried (powdered) yeast

METHOD

Place the flour and 400 ml (14 fl oz) of water in a mixer with a dough hook attachment. Dissolve the yeast in the remaining water.

Turn on the mixer at its lowest speed and add the dissolved yeast. Keep working until a rough dough is produced. It may take 5–6 minutes. It doesn't need to be smooth; it just needs to hold together in a rough mass.

Place the dough in a clean plastic bucket, glass or ceramic container, cover with plastic wrap or a lid and keep at a temperature between 16–20°C (60–68°F) for 16–18 hours.

FOR THE FINAL DOUGH

300 g (10½ oz) biga (the first dough)
1 kg (2 lb 4 oz/6⅔ cups) unbleached, stoneground
    whole-wheat flour or strong bread flour
550 ml (19 fl oz) water at correct temperature
    (see temperature note opposite)
35 g (1¼ oz) sea salt
35 ml (1¼ fl oz) extra virgin olive oil

METHOD

Place all the ingredients except the olive oil in a mixer fitted with a dough hook attachment. Work at the lowest speed for 8 minutes. When the dough is homogenous, increase the speed slightly and work for about 20 minutes or so until the gluten has developed to the point where the dough can be stretched like bubble gum.

Finally, add the olive oil and mix for 1 minute. Turn the dough onto a work surface, cover with plastic wrap and leave at ambient temperature for 30 minutes in winter or 15 minutes in summer. The dough is now ready to be shaped into balls and then rested further in the refrigerator before shaping into discs (see pages 80–83).

Makes 6 pizze (250 g/9 oz each)

Temperature

The temperature of the final dough produced by the indirect method is important. It should be less than 24°C (75°F).

Temperature is key in controlling the activity of yeast and influencing dough structure. It prevents the formation of large air bubbles and promotes the elasticity of the dough. It can be achieved by controlling the temperature (T) of the water added to the final dough by using a simple formula:

$T_{water} = 3T_{dough} - (T_{ambient} + T_{flour} + T_{machine\ bowl})$

So, to find out the correct water temperature (T_{water}), multiply the dough temperature by 3 ($3T_{dough}$). Now add together the temperature of the room, of the flour and of the mixer machine bowl ($T_{ambient} + T_{flour} + T_{machine\ bowl}$). Take this number away from the $3T_{dough}$ and you'll have the temperature of the water to be added.

To measure these temperatures we use a combination of a normal thermometer, a probe thermometer (for the dough and flour) and an infrared gun thermometer. This last one is used for the machine bowl, though if the mixer is kept in the kitchen it's probably ambient temperature.

As an example, if the dough temperature required is 22°C, ambient 24°C, flour 18°C and machine bowl 20°C, the formula would look like this:

$T_{water} = 3 \times 22°C - (24°C + 18°C + 20°C)$ or $T_{water} = 66°C - 62°C$

Therefore the water temperature needs to be 4°C when added. This will be the temperature of water kept in a refrigerator. If lower temperatures are required, then ice added to a little refrigerated water is fine.

Spelt pizza dough

Patrick Ricci, whose meticulous research with spelt flours has been rewarded with some of the most outstanding pizza dough I've ever tasted, has kindly given me this recipe. Even though he works with these difficult flours every day, even he has days when a flour does not respond as it should, or as it did the last time. He describes the taming of these flours as like trying to tame a crazy horse. But the rewards are immense.

Making 100 per cent spelt dough is extremely difficult because it's a fairly weak flour. I have included this recipe as an advanced procedure for those who want a challenge. It will require research into flour sources and patience. The resultant pizza won't have the large, puffy cornice of the basic pizza dough, but will have a crisper, nuttier and more complex base. It's important to remember that each country has different sources of flours, so if you are buying spelt flour, make sure it is Triticum spelta.

INGREDIENTS

1 g (1/25 oz) dried (powdered) yeast or 250 g (9 oz) Sourdough starter (see page opposite)
550 ml (19 fl oz) water, at a temperature between 4–7°C (39–45°F) – refrigerator temperature
1 kg (2 lb 4 oz) stoneground 'white' spelt flour
22 g (3/4 oz) sea salt

METHOD

If using yeast, dissolve the yeast in 500 ml (17 fl oz/2 cups) of water (keeping the remaining water aside and cold). If using the sourdough starter, it can be added once refreshed and activated.

Place the flour and water (with the yeast) in a mixer with a dough hook attachment and mix at a low speed for 5 minutes.

Mix the rest of the water in a bowl with the salt and add to the dough. Turn on the mixer and mix at the same low speed for 15 minutes. Place the dough in a plastic container with an airtight lid and keep in the refrigerator for 24 hours.

Remove the dough to a work surface and knead, stretch and fold for 5–8 minutes, then return to the refrigerator in the covered container for 4 hours. Repeat twice more. After the final fold, place in a refrigerator set at 10°C (50°F) – a wine cabinet is handy if available. Keep at this temperature for about 12–15 hours, after which you can form the dough into six dough balls (see pages 80–81). Once shaped into balls and placed in a covered container, go straight to the next step below, rather than following Step 6 on page 81.

Place the dough balls in the refrigerator at 4–6°C (39–43°F) for 4 hours. Remove from the refrigerator to ambient temperature for a couple of hours before forming the pizze (see pages 82–83, Steps 2–8).

Makes around 6 pizze (250 g/9 oz each)

Sourdough starter (lievito madre)

This starter is used instead of commercial yeast and will impart a unique flavour to your pizze that is all your own. It's important to use stone-milled flour as it has the vitality and nutrients to attract the good yeasts present in the air. Yoghurt also helps to activate the process because it's fermented.

FOR THE FIRST DOUGH

300 g (10½ oz/2 cups) unbleached, stoneground whole-wheat flour or strong bread flour, plus a little more if needed
300 g (10½ oz/1¼ cups) natural yoghurt

Place the flour in a ceramic or glass bowl. Add the yoghurt and mix together using your hands. Once the mass has come together, remove from the bowl and place on a work surface.

Knead for about 2–3 minutes until the dough has come together and is not too wet and not too dry. It shouldn't be sticky. Add a little more flour if necessary. Place back in the glass or ceramic bowl, seal with plastic wrap and prick five or six holes in the wrap to allow gasses to exit. Leave to activate on the work surface, not in direct sunlight, at a temperature between 24–28°C (75–82°F) for 48 hours.

FOR THE FIRST REFRESH

250 g (9 oz) of the first dough
250 g (9 oz/1⅔ cups) unbleached, stoneground whole-wheat flour or strong bread flour
125 ml (4 fl oz/½ cup) water

After 48 hours your dough should be activated. You'll be able to see that it has become a little more liquid and, if it's in a glass bowl, that bubbles have formed internally. Remove the plastic wrap and, using your fingers, pinch the thin crust that will have formed on the surface from the outer edge to the centre, lift it out and discard.

In a new glass or ceramic bowl, weigh 250 g (9 oz) of the dough and discard the rest. Add the flour and all but 30 ml (1 fl oz) of the water. Mix using your hands. If the dough is too dry, add a little more water. Once the mass has come together, place on a work surface and knead for 2–3 minutes. It should be smooth and even, similar to the first dough.

Place the dough in a clean 2 litre (70 fl oz) tall jar with a wide opening. The high, straight sides will help the dough gain strength. Arrange the dough on the bottom of the jar, making sure there are no air bubbles underneath. Cover the jar with some muslin (cheesecloth), secured with an elastic band. Leave for 24 hours at a temperature between 22–26°C (72–79°F).

FOR THE SUBSEQUENT REFRESHES / Repeat the first refresh for 14 more days, always taking 250 g (9 oz) of the clean dough from the previous day and proceeding with the same quantities of flour and water. This constant refresh will gradually strengthen the dough.

On the fifteenth day, refresh as usual. Place the dough in a large glass jar but instead of covering with permeable muslin (cheesecloth), close with a tight lid so no air gets in and no gas gets out. If the dough rises and increases in volume by a factor of three or more, your lievito madre, or natural starter, is strong enough to use.

Before using your natural starter in any dough recipe, it's important to do a quick refresh and leave for 4–5 hours to activate. Refresh in these proportions: mix 1 part starter, 1 part flour and 1 part water.

MAINTAINING THE DOUGH / Keep the dough in the fridge, completely sealed. You can build up the quantity of natural starter by now keeping more of each refresh. If kept in the fridge you'll have to feed (refresh) the dough once every 4–5 days.

When you need to use the natural starter, remove from the refrigerator and take the amount needed before you refresh. Make sure that any crust that forms is removed.

If using in the recipes in this book, instead of the commercial yeast, add 25 per cent of this starter by weight to the total flour amount. For example, if the flour quantity is 1 kg (2 lb 4 oz/6⅔ cups), then add 250 g (9 oz) of natural starter and proceed as normal.

Shaping basic dough into balls

Once the dough is ready to be shaped, take a bench scraper and cut off a piece from the edge.

The dough will feel soft, airy and malleable. Take the piece of dough at one end and, using both hands, form a ball about 200–250 g (7–9 oz) in size. Work by tucking the folds under the ball so that the top surface is taut and smooth.

Pinch the dough underneath the formed ball to separate it from the long piece of dough.

Repeat this procedure to make more balls.

Roll each ball gently on the work surface to make it even and round.

Place the balls on a covered non-stick tray. Make sure there is at least one ball width between each ball and the edges of the tray and that the balls don't touch the cover. Use a fine mist water spray to hydrate the surface of the balls once they are on the tray. Let rise for 1 hour at 20–24°C (68–75°F). After resting, place in a refrigerator for at least 12 hours and up to 18 hours. The balls can sit in the refrigerator at around 4–5°C (39–41°F) for up to 3 days.

Shaping basic dough into bases

Once the dough has matured and tripled in size, remove from the refrigerator and leave at ambient temperature for 3–4 hours (less in summer and more in winter) before forming the bases. Choose the dough ball to be used and lightly sprinkle some flour on top and along the edges where it touches the surrounding balls.

Use the bench scraper to separate the dough ball from its neighbours.

Lift the dough ball from the tray and turn bottom side up, revealing the bubbles.

Place the dough ball, still bottom side up, on a small mound of flour and turn it over in the flour so that both sides are covered.

Begin by using your fingers to form the cornice (border) and push the dough out, making the circle larger.

Once it has doubled in circumference, remove from the flour and place on the work surface.

Keeping one hand on one side of the base, gently stretch the opposite side with the other hand and lift and slap the dough circle from side to side. This will stretch the gluten in the dough and the base will get larger and larger.

Once stretched to the desired size (our pizze are around 30 cm/ 12 inches in diameter), place the base back on the work surface and neaten into a circle. The pizza base is now ready to dress with the toppings and then bake.

Roman-style pizza dough Basic

Roman-style pizza is a rectangular, focaccia-like pizza that is famous in Rome. It is light, full of large bubbles and can be filled or topped with many ingredients. Roman-style pizza does not require a wood-fired oven, but traditionally is cooked in a 'deck' oven at almost half the temperature of wood-fired pizza. Use stoneground whole-wheat (not wholemeal) flour.

INGREDIENTS

1 kg (2 lb 4 oz/6⅔ cups) unbleached, stoneground whole-wheat flour or strong bread flour
3.5 g (⅛ oz) dried (powdered) yeast or 125 g (4½ oz) Sourdough starter (see page 79)
650 ml (23 fl oz) water at room temperature
½ teaspoon caster (superfine) sugar
25 ml (1 fl oz) extra virgin olive oil
20 g (¾ oz) sea salt

METHOD

Place the flour in a mixer with a dough hook attachment.

Dissolve the yeast in 100 ml (3½ fl oz) of the water (or if using the sourdough starter, remove 50 ml (1¾ fl oz) of water from the recipe and simply add the starter) and add to the flour along with 400 ml (14 fl oz) of the remaining water and the caster sugar.

Turn on the mixer to its lowest setting and mix for about 2 minutes until the water is totally absorbed. Add the oil and salt and mix in. Double the speed of the mixer and slowly add the remaining water, a little at a time, only adding more when the previous amount has been absorbed. The mixture will look quite wet, but don't worry, continue mixing for 8–10 minutes and you'll see that gradually the dough will begin to stretch and form long gluten strands.

Rest the dough for 10 minutes in the mixer bowl, covered with plastic wrap, before folding, leaving to mature in the refrigerator and forming into three sheets (teglie) of Roman-style pizza dough (see pages 86–88).

Makes 3 teglie (550 g/1 lb 4 oz sheets)

Roman-style pizza dough Mixed wheat

This recipe produces a full-flavoured, fragrant Roman-style pizza dough and can be substituted for the basic Roman-style pizza dough quite successfully in any recipe. The method is based on a recipe from Gabriele Bonci. Once again, the flours used are the most important factor. The best results are obtained by using stoneground, whole-wheat types. I use Italian flours such as Petra or Mulino Marino, but any good whole-wheat flour will work well.

INGREDIENTS

500 g (1 lb 2 oz/3⅓ cups) unbleached, stoneground whole-wheat flour or strong bread flour
200 g (7 oz/1⅓ cups) wholemeal flour
200 g (7 oz/2 cups) stoneground 'white' spelt flour
100 g (3½ oz/¾ cup) rye flour
3 g (⅛ oz) dried (powdered) yeast or 125 g (4½ oz) Sourdough starter (see page 79)
800 ml (28 fl oz) water at room temperature
25 ml (1 fl oz) extra virgin olive oil
15 g (½ oz) sea salt

METHOD

Mix all the flours together in a mixer with a beater attachment.

In a small bowl, dissolve the yeast in 50 ml (1¾ fl oz) water (or if using the sourdough starter, remove 50 ml (1¾ fl oz) of water from the recipe and simply add the starter). Add this, along with 550 ml (19 fl oz) of the water, the oil and salt to the flour and mix on the lowest speed. Once the dough comes together, change the beater attachment to the dough attachment, double the mixer speed and continue mixing, adding the rest of the water, a little at a time, until it's all absorbed. The mixture will look quite wet, but don't worry, continue mixing for 8–10 minutes and you'll see that gradually the dough will begin to stretch and form long gluten strands.

Rest the dough for 10 minutes in the mixer bowl, covered with plastic wrap, before folding, leaving to mature in the refrigerator and forming into three sheets (teglie) of Roman-style pizza dough (see pages 86–88).

Makes 3 teglie (550 g/1 lb 4 oz sheets)

Shaping Roman-style dough

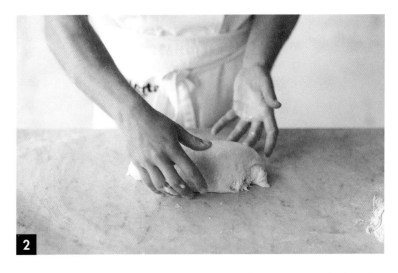

FOLDING / Once the dough has been briefly rested, it needs to be folded a few times to give it strength. Oil your hands with a teaspoon of extra virgin olive oil, then lightly oil the work surface. Tip the dough out of the container and onto the work surface. Lift it gently in the centre and fold the ends under (or over) to meet in the middle to form pockets of air.

Turn the dough 90 degrees and repeat the fold. Return to the bowl, cover with plastic wrap and rest for 15 minutes, then fold again. Rest for another 15 minutes, then do a final fold as before. Place the dough in an oiled, plastic container with an airtight lid and leave for 18–24 hours in the refrigerator.

Once the dough has matured in the refrigerator, turn out from the container on to the work surface. Divide the dough into three pieces.

Shape each piece of dough. Place your hands under the outer edges and slide under to form a ball. Repeat several times until the dough has a ball-like appearance.

Fold and gather with your fingers at the edge of each piece of dough, bringing the ball towards you. This will eventually make the ball even and smooth. The dough balls should be left to rise again in three oiled containers for 2 hours at room temperature.

STRETCHING / Oil an oven tray (teglia) or baking tray with extra virgin olive oil.

Place flour on the work surface and turn one piece of the dough.

Begin to press gently on the surface of the dough with your fingers, stretching it to roughly fit the size of the tray.

Transfer the dough to the baking tray, gently supporting the dough with as much of your arms as possible.

Stretch the dough gently to fit and then make delicate indents on the surface with your fingers.

Sprinkle some extra virgin olive oil on the surface and then gently spread it with your fingers. The pizza is now ready to be dressed with toppings or to go directly into the oven to be precooked.

Cooking basic dough

Shaped and topped, here you'll find instructions for cooking your round pizze.

In a wood-fired oven

With the floor temperature between 360–400°C (680–750°F), a pizza will take around 90 seconds to cook. Some pizzaioli cook at temperatures up to 450°C (840°F) and this takes less time. The pizza is put directly on to the oven floor to cook, thereby getting an immediate 'lift'.

In a domestic oven

My suggestion is to find a large terracotta tile that fits onto your oven rack. Place the rack on the bottom rung of your oven and the tile on top, giving you plenty of room above to manipulate the pizza. Turn to full heat without using any fan-forced function and let the oven run for at least 20 minutes to heat the tile completely. When the pizza is ready, use a floured paddle to take it from the bench on to the tile. Close the oven immediately.

At around 250–280°C (480–535°F) a pizza takes 3–5 minutes to cook, depending on your oven temperature. It will have a crisp, bread-like texture and should be no less delicious than the wood-fired version.

Cooking Roman-style dough

Roman-style pizza is often precooked. It's convenient because the cooked dough can be kept in the fridge and brought out, topped and heated in the oven when needed.

Preheat the oven to 250°C (500°F) without fan.

Take the sheet of Roman-style pizza dough and if the dough has risen excessively, press down gently with the tips of your fingers to make small indentations.

Bake the pizza in the oven for 11–14 minutes. If the teglia is browning more on one side, your oven is not even and the tray may need to be turned.

Once cooked, remove from the oven and let cool a little before dressing with your toppings or allow to cool completely if using later. The teglia can be wrapped tightly with plastic wrap and stored in the refrigerator for up to 3 days.

Literally translated, 'pizza rossa' means 'red pizza'. These are the pizze that have puréed tomato as a base for the topping. I use San Marzano DOP from a producer (Danicoop) I trust and whom I've visited (see page 21). There are other good tomatoes that can also be used from areas such as Sardinia, Puglia and Sicily. The essential qualities to seek out are ripeness, colour, flavour and the ability to not release water when cooking.

Marinara Napoletana

This is the classic, and perhaps original, Neapolitan pizza. There are few ingredients – no cheese and no seafood!

INGREDIENTS

250 g (9 oz) ball of basic pizza dough
    (see pages 74–77), shaped
    (see pages 80–83)

100 g (3½ oz/⅓ cup) tinned
    San Marzano whole peeled tomatoes
A pinch of sea salt
1 garlic clove, crushed
2 tablespoons extra virgin olive oil
2–3 good pinches of best-quality
    dried oregano
1 garlic clove, thinly sliced

METHOD

TO ASSEMBLE / Place a large tile in your oven for the pizza, then preheat to full heat (without using any fan-forced function) for at least 20 minutes (see page 89). Squeeze the tomatoes by hand or with a fork until they're uniformly mashed and mix in a pinch of salt. Mix the crushed garlic and olive oil together. Spread the mashed tomato onto the shaped pizza base, leaving the edges clear to about 3–4 cm (1½ inches). Scatter the dried oregano over the tomato. Drizzle half the oil and garlic mixture over the tomato. Distribute the garlic slices here and there. Place the pizza in the oven for 3–5 minutes until cooked, turning to get an even colour. Remove and drizzle with the remaining oil.

Makes one 30 cm (12 inch) pizza

Margherita

Along with the Marinara, the Margherita represents the classic pizza of Naples. In fact, there are still places that only serve these two pizze. The Margherita is perhaps the world's most iconic pizza.

INGREDIENTS

250 g (9 oz) ball of basic pizza dough
    (see pages 74–77), shaped
    (see pages 80–83)

80–100 g (3–3½ oz/⅓ cup) tinned
    San Marzano whole peeled tomatoes
150 g (5½ oz) fior di latte mozzarella
A handful of fresh basil leaves
1 tablespoon extra virgin olive oil

METHOD

TO ASSEMBLE / Place a large tile in your oven for the pizza, then preheat to full heat (without using any fan-forced function) for at least 20 minutes (see page 89). Hand squeeze the tomatoes; it doesn't matter if there are pieces left and they're not completely uniform. Spread onto the shaped pizza base, leaving the edges clear to about 3–4 cm (1½ inches). Thinly slice the mozzarella and scatter evenly, here and there, on the tomato. Place the basil leaves on top. Place the pizza in the oven for 3–5 minutes until cooked, turning to get an even colour. Remove and drizzle with the oil.

Makes one 30 cm (12 inch) pizza

Chargrilled vegetables

The vegetables on this pizza can (and should) change with the seasons. Leeks would work well in winter or thin slices of squash or pumpkin. Similarly, asparagus in spring and string beans in summer go nicely, as would any vegetable that can be chargrilled.

INGREDIENTS

250 g (9 oz) ball of basic pizza dough
(see pages 74–77), shaped
(see pages 80–83)

1 red onion, skin left on, halved
80 g (3 oz/⅓ cup) tinned San Marzano
whole peeled tomatoes
150 g (5½ oz) fior di latte mozzarella
50 g (2 oz/½ cup) grated parmesan
cheese

CHARGRILLED VEGETABLES

1 zucchini (courgette), trimmed and cut
lengthways into 3 mm (⅛ inch) slices
½ eggplant (aubergine), trimmed and cut
into 3 mm (⅛ inch) slices
Sea salt and freshly ground black pepper
Extra virgin olive oil

METHOD

TO ASSEMBLE / Season all the vegetable slices except the onion, add a little extra virgin olive oil and chargrill for about 30 seconds on each side until tender. Brush the onion with olive oil and place in a 200°C (400°F) oven for about 15–20 minutes or until tender all the way to the centre. Remove the outer skin and tough leaves of flesh and separate out the tender flesh to use on the pizza.

Place a large tile in your oven for the pizza, then turn the oven up to preheat to full heat (without using any fan-forced function) for at least 20 minutes (see page 89). Hand squeeze the tomatoes; it doesn't matter if there are pieces left and they're not completely uniform. Spread onto the shaped pizza base, leaving the edges clear to about 3–4 cm (1½ inches). Thinly slice the mozzarella and scatter evenly, here and there, on the tomato. Scatter the grated parmesan and then the vegetables evenly over the surface, making sure not to pile too much on. Place in the oven for 3–5 minutes until cooked, turning to get an even colour. Remove and drizzle with 1 tablespoon of the extra virgin olive oil.

Makes one 30 cm (12 inch) pizza

OPPOSITE / A Cetara fisherman mending his nets. **THIS PAGE** / The seaside town of Cetara, on the southern side of the Sorrentine Peninsula, south of Naples.

Sicilian capers and anchovies

This is the pizza for the anchovy lover. It combines all those salty, sea-breezy flavours of the Mediterranean. Remember to use the best ingredients, especially the capers. They should be salted, not pickled.

INGREDIENTS

250 g (9 oz) ball of basic pizza dough
  (see pages 74–77), shaped
  (see pages 80–83)

80 g (3 oz/⅓ cup) tinned San Marzano
  whole peeled tomatoes
100 g (3½ oz) fior di latte mozzarella
2 tablespoons Sicilian capers, soaked and
  desalted (see page 36)
6 large or 12 small anchovies
12 Gaeta (or similar) black olives, pitted
2–3 pinches of best-quality dried oregano
A pinch of sea salt
1 tablespoon extra virgin olive oil

METHOD

TO ASSEMBLE / Place a large tile in your oven for the pizza, then preheat to full heat (without using any fan-forced function) for at least 20 minutes (see page 89). Hand squeeze the tomatoes. It doesn't matter if there are pieces left and they're not completely uniform. Spread onto the shaped pizza base, leaving the edges clear to about 3–4 cm (1½ inches). Thinly slice the mozzarella and scatter evenly, here and there, on the tomato. Scatter with the desalted capers and place the anchovies evenly over the pizza. Do the same with the olives and oregano. Season with a little salt and cook the pizza in the oven for 3–5 minutes until cooked, turning to get an even colour. Once out of the oven, drizzle with the olive oil.

Makes one 30 cm (12 inch) pizza

Smoked leg ham, mushroom and sage

This is a lovely combination of flavours, especially between the smoked leg ham and the sage. Don't buy pre-packaged ham, but rather have it sliced off the bone and ask for it a little thicker for texture.

INGREDIENTS

250 g (9 oz) ball of basic pizza dough
(see pages 74–77), shaped
(see pages 80–83)

50 ml (2 fl oz/¼ cup) extra virgin olive oil,
for frying, plus 1 tablespoon for
drizzling
12 large fresh sage leaves
80 g (3 oz/⅓ cup) tinned San Marzano
whole peeled tomatoes
100 g (3½ oz) fior di latte mozzarella
90 g (3½ oz) smoked leg ham, shaved
90 g (3½ oz/1 cup) thinly sliced button or
small cap mushrooms
Sea salt and freshly ground black pepper

METHOD

TO ASSEMBLE / Place a large tile in your oven for the pizza, then preheat to full heat (without using any fan-forced function) for at least 20 minutes (see page 89). Heat the extra virgin olive oil in a small saucepan and fry the sage leaves until crisp. Remove from the oil and drain on some paper towel.

Hand squeeze the tomatoes; it doesn't matter if there are pieces left and they're not completely uniform. Spread the squeezed tomato onto the shaped pizza base, leaving the edges clear to about 3–4 cm (1½ inches). Thinly slice the mozzarella and scatter evenly, here and there, on the tomato. Scatter the ham and mushrooms evenly over the pizza. Season with a little salt and a couple of turns of the pepper mill and cook in the oven for 3–5 minutes until cooked, turning to get an even colour. Once out of the oven, drizzle with the remaining olive oil and scatter the fried sage on top.

Makes one 30 cm (12 inch) pizza

Tuna, Mediterranean herbs and colatura

Colatura is the ancient fish sauce the Romans once used and it is still being made from salted anchovies in Cetara on the Amalfi Coast, south of Naples.

INGREDIENTS

250 g (9 oz) ball of basic pizza dough
   (see pages 74–77), shaped
   (see pages 80–83)

1 tablespoon extra virgin olive oil
1 teaspoon colatura d'alici
1 small garlic clove, crushed
1 tablespoon fresh basil, finely chopped
1 tablespoon fresh parsley, finely chopped
½ teaspoon best-quality dried oregano
160 g (5½ oz) piece of tuna, cut into
   1 cm (½ inch) cubes
80 g (3 oz/⅓ cup) tinned San Marzano
   whole peeled tomatoes
80 g (3 oz) fior di latte mozzarella
½ red onion, thinly sliced
10 Gaeta (or similar) black olives, pitted
1 tablespoon Sicilian capers, soaked and
   desalted (see page 36)

METHOD

TO ASSEMBLE / Place a large tile in your oven for the pizza, then preheat to full heat (without using any fan-forced function) for at least 20 minutes (see page 89). Mix the olive oil, colatura and garlic together and set apart in a small bowl. Next, mix the chopped basil and parsley with the dried oregano and toss with the tuna cubes until they're well coated and set aside.

Hand squeeze the tomatoes; it doesn't matter if there are pieces left and they're not completely uniform. Spread the squeezed tomato onto the shaped pizza base, leaving the edges clear to 3–4 cm (1½ inches). Thinly slice the mozzarella and scatter evenly, here and there, on top of the tomato. Scatter the onion around and place the herbed tuna cubes on top along with the olives and capers. Place the pizza in the oven for 3–5 minutes until cooked, turning to get an even colour. Remove and drizzle with the oil, garlic and colatura mixture.

Makes one 30 cm (12 inch) pizza

Calamari, chilli and ginger

This is a combination I use in various dishes and it works well on this pizza. In fact, the most recent ingredient in this combination to arrive in Europe is the chilli. Ginger was used extensively by the Romans not only as a digestive, but as a flavouring too.

INGREDIENTS

250 g (9 oz) ball of basic pizza dough (see pages 74–77), shaped (see pages 80–83)

2 tablespoons extra virgin olive oil
180 g (6½ oz) cleaned calamari (squid), patted dry with paper towel
1 garlic clove, crushed
1–2 chillies, finely sliced
1 teaspoon finely chopped fresh ginger
Sea salt
1 tablespoon finely chopped fresh parsley
80 g (3 oz/⅓ cup) tinned San Marzano whole peeled tomatoes
80 g (3 oz) fior di latte mozzarella

METHOD

TO ASSEMBLE / Place a large tile in your oven for the pizza, then preheat to full heat (without using any fan-forced function) for at least 20 minutes (see page 89). Heat the olive oil in a heavy-based frying pan. Once it starts to smoke, carefully add the calamari, garlic, chilli and ginger. Fry over a high heat for a minute or so until just cooked. Season with salt, mix in the parsley and set aside to cool. Once cool, drain any oil or liquid from the calamari and reserve.

Hand squeeze the tomatoes; it doesn't matter if there are pieces left and they're not completely uniform. Spread the squeezed tomato onto the shaped pizza base, leaving the edges clear to 3–4 cm (1½ inches). Thinly slice the mozzarella and scatter evenly, here and there, on top of the tomato. Scatter the calamari over the mozzarella. Place in the oven for 3–5 minutes until cooked, turning to get an even colour. Remove and drizzle with a tablespoon of the reserved oil.

Makes one 30 cm (12 inch) pizza

THIS PAGE / An Amalfi Coast fisherman showing off a highly prized octopus.

PIZ
BIA

Literally translated, 'pizza bianca' means 'white pizza' because it doesn't have puréed tomato as the base topping. A pizza bianca is often lighter and, without the dominating tomato, it is open to many more ingredients that can be used as toppings.

Prawns, zucchini and mint

All great pizza begins with the best ingredients. This one has to have the best prawns you can find.

INGREDIENTS

250 g (9 oz) ball of basic pizza dough
   (see pages 74–77), shaped
   (see pages 80–83)

2 tablespoons chopped fresh mint leaves
3 tablespoons extra virgin olive oil, plus
   extra for brushing
1 zucchini (courgette), trimmed and cut
   lengthways into 3 mm (⅛ inch) thick
   slices
Sea salt and freshly ground black pepper
150 g (5½ oz) fior di latte mozzarella
4–5 large king prawns (shrimp), shelled,
   deveined and sliced in half lengthways

METHOD

TO ASSEMBLE / Marinate the chopped mint in the olive oil for an hour or so before making the pizza, then strain the leaves, keeping the oil. Season the zucchini, add a little extra virgin olive oil and chargrill for about 30 seconds on each side until tender.

Place a large tile in your oven for the pizza, then turn the oven up to preheat to full heat (without using any fan-forced function) for at least 20 minutes (see page 89). Thinly slice the mozzarella and scatter evenly, here and there, to top the shaped pizza base, leaving the edges clear to about 3–4 cm (1½ inches). Scatter the zucchini and prawn halves over the pizza so that each eventual pizza slice contains some. Place in the oven for 3–5 minutes until cooked, turning to get an even colour. Remove and drizzle with the mint oil.

Makes one 30 cm (12 inch) pizza

Hot calabrese

This pizza calls for a smoked cheese called provola and a typical Calabrese spreadable sausage called 'nduja. The Gaeta olive is a medium-sized black olive from south of Rome, renowned for its plump, meaty texture and excellent tart, salty flavour.

INGREDIENTS

250 g (9 oz) ball of basic pizza dough
   (see pages 74–77), shaped
   (see pages 80–83)

2 best-quality Italian-style pork and fennel
   sausages
1 tablespoon 'nduja
100 g (3½ oz) smoked provola cheese
10 cherry tomatoes, halved
1 red or yellow capsicum (pepper),
   trimmed, deseeded and chopped into
   long strips
10 Gaeta (or similar) black olives, pitted
Sea salt
1 tablespoon extra virgin olive oil

METHOD

TO ASSEMBLE / Place a large tile in your oven for the pizza, then turn the oven up to preheat to full heat (without using any fan-forced function) for at least 20 minutes (see page 89). Cut the skin and remove the meat from the sausages. Place in a bowl with the 'nduja. Mix well with hands or a fork. Thinly slice the smoked provola and scatter evenly, here and there, to top the shaped pizza base, leaving the edges clear to about 3–4 cm (1½ inches).

Add the sausage and 'nduja mixture evenly in dollops using a teaspoon. Finally, scatter the cherry tomatoes, capsicum slices and olives over the pizza. Season with a pinch of salt. Place the pizza in the oven for 3–5 minutes until cooked, turning to get an even colour. Remove and drizzle with the olive oil.

Makes one 30 cm (12 inch) pizza.

Frutti di mare (seafood) and avocado

Many people believe that a seafood pizza is a 'Marinara'. It's not. A Marinara pizza is the simplest of all pizze with tomato, garlic, oregano and extra virgin olive oil. A seafood pizza is a 'Frutti di mare'. We have a version of this seafood pizza on the menu at all times.

INGREDIENTS

250 g (9 oz) ball of basic pizza dough
(see pages 74–77), shaped
(see pages 80–83)

3 large scallops, halved
3 large king prawns (shrimp), shelled,
deveined and sliced in half lengthways
70 g (2½ oz) cleaned calamari (squid),
sliced into 5 x 1 cm (2 x ½ inch)
pieces, patted dry with paper towel
1 tablespoon extra virgin olive oil, plus
1 teaspoon for the avocado
1 garlic clove, crushed
Sea salt and freshly ground black pepper
½ avocado, flesh removed
Juice of 1 lime
2 tablespoons chopped fresh parsley
100 g (3½ oz) fior di latte mozzarella
10 cherry tomatoes, quartered

METHOD

TO ASSEMBLE / Place a large tile in your oven for the pizza, then turn the oven up to preheat to full heat (without using any fan-forced function) for at least 20 minutes (see page 89).

Prepare all the seafood first so it is ready to go on your pizza. Scallops and prawns can go on raw as they will cook quickly on the pizza. The calamari needs to be cooked briefly first by heating a tablespoon of extra virgin olive oil in a small heavy-based frying pan and tossing the calamari in over a high heat with the crushed garlic. Season with salt and pepper and fry for about 30 seconds. Remove from the pan into a cold bowl with all the juices. Place the avocado flesh in a small bowl with the lime juice, half the parsley, a pinch of salt and pepper and a teaspoon of extra virgin olive oil. Mash with a fork until smooth. Place in a piping bag in the refrigerator.

Thinly slice the mozzarella and scatter evenly, here and there, to top the shaped pizza base, leaving the edges clear to about 3–4 cm (1½ inches). Scatter the seafood over the mozzarella, reserving the oil from the cooked calamari. Distribute the tomato quarters over the surface. Place the pizza in the oven for 3–5 minutes until cooked, turning to get an even colour. Remove, drizzle the calamari oil on top and pipe a little avocado next to each of the six slices of scallop. Finish by scattering the rest of the parsley on top.

Makes one 30 cm (12 inch) pizza

Ceci – chickpeas, eggplant and salted ricotta

This pizza uses salted ricotta (ricotta salata), which is firm enough to grate and adds a salty, snow-like finish that looks and tastes wonderful. The chickpeas are puréed, adding flavour without their often mealy texture.

INGREDIENTS

250 g (9 oz) ball of basic pizza dough
   (see pages 74–77), shaped
   (see pages 80–83)

100 g (3½ oz) fior di latte mozzarella
25 g (1 oz/¼ cup) thinly sliced leek
8–12 slices of chargrilled eggplant
   (aubergine) (see page 98)
A handful of confit tomatoes (see
   page 152)
1 tablespoon toasted pine nuts
2 tablespoons grated salted ricotta cheese

CHICKPEA PUREE

200 g (7 oz/1 cup) dried chickpeas
125 ml (4 fl oz/½ cup) extra virgin olive oil
1 garlic clove, crushed
A pinch of best-quality dried oregano
Salt and freshly ground black pepper

METHOD

FOR THE CHICKPEA PUREE / Soak the chickpeas in abundant cold water for 24 hours. Drain well and wash the chickpeas to get rid of any skins that come off. Place in a pot and cover with cold water to a level of 6 cm (2½ inches) above the chickpeas. Bring the pot to the boil. Immediately turn down to a low simmer and cover with a lid. Keep simmering very gently for 2–3 hours until the chickpeas are soft and tender. Drain, but keep a cup of the cooking liquid. Place the cooked chickpeas in a blender with the olive oil, garlic and oregano. Pulse until smooth. Season to taste with salt and pepper. The purée should be thick enough to pipe. If it's too thick, add a little of the cooking water. Any left-over purée will keep for up to a week, covered, in the refrigerator.

TO ASSEMBLE / Place a large tile in your oven for the pizza, then turn the oven up to preheat to full heat (without using any fan-forced function) for at least 20 minutes (see page 89). Thinly slice the mozzarella and scatter evenly, here and there, to top the shaped pizza base, leaving the edges clear to about 3–4 cm (1½ inches). Scatter the leek and eggplant evenly over the pizza. Place the pizza in the oven for 3–5 minutes until cooked, turning to get an even colour. Once out of the oven, scatter with the confit tomatoes. Using a piping bag, pipe on the chickpea purée here and there, in dollops or strips, over the pizza. Add the pine nuts and salted ricotta.

Makes one 30 cm (12 inch) pizza

Capocollo and fennel

Capocollo is pork neck, salted and dried like prosciutto. Some of the very best comes from around the city of Martina Franca in Puglia. Most good Italian butchers will make their own version.

INGREDIENTS

250 g (9 oz) ball of basic pizza dough
  (see pages 74–77), shaped
  (see pages 80–83)

100 g (3½ oz) fior di latte mozzarella
70 g (2½ oz/½ cup) thinly sliced fennel,
  plus 8 fennel fronds
8 slices of capocollo di Martina Franca
2 tablespoons grated pecorino cheese
1 tablespoon extra virgin olive oil
A couple of pinches of freshly ground
  black pepper

METHOD

TO ASSEMBLE / Place a large tile in your oven for the pizza, then turn the oven up to preheat to full heat (without using any fan-forced function) for at least 20 minutes (see page 89). Thinly slice the mozzarella and scatter evenly, here and there, to top the shaped pizza base, leaving the edges clear to about 3–4 cm (1½ inches). Scatter the fennel evenly over the pizza. Place the pizza in the oven for 3–5 minutes until cooked, turning to get an even colour. Once out of the oven, place the capocollo slices over the pizza. Sprinkle the pecorino on top and distribute the fennel fronds over the lot. Drizzle with the olive oil and add a little black pepper.

Makes one 30 cm (12 inch) pizza

Chicory, salame and stracciatella

Stracciatella is a mixture of fine mozzarella strands mixed with cream. It can be used by itself and is featured as the filling in the extraordinary burrata cheese, originating in Puglia. Chicory is native to the Mediterranean region and is widely used, raw and cooked, in various dishes. It is bitter, but cooking the green leaves removes much of the bitterness.

INGREDIENTS

250 g (9 oz) ball of basic pizza dough
   (see pages 74–77), shaped
   (see pages 80–83)

100 g (3½ oz) fior di latte mozzarella
6 slices of good-quality Italian salame,
   sliced and cut into 'straws'
1 tablespoon grated parmesan cheese
4 tablespoons stracciatella cheese
A handful of confit tomatoes
   (see page 152)
1 tablespoon extra virgin olive oil
A couple of pinches of freshly ground
   black pepper

COOKED CHICORY
1 tablespoon salt
500 g (1 lb 2 oz) chicory leaves
1 tablespoon extra virgin olive oil
1 garlic clove, lightly crushed
Sea salt

METHOD

FOR THE COOKED CHICORY / Bring 5 litres (175 fl oz/20 cups) of water to the boil in a pot with a tablespoon of salt added. Plunge in the chicory and submerge with a wooden spoon. After the water returns to the boil, cook the chicory for 3–4 minutes. Drain and let the leaves cool to room temperature. Squeeze as much water out of the leaves as possible. Place the chicory leaves on a board and roughly chop, then put in a bowl and add the olive oil, garlic clove and a little salt. Mix thoroughly. Any leftover chicory can be kept in the refrigerator for up to a week.

TO ASSEMBLE / Place a large tile in your oven for the pizza, then turn the oven up to preheat to full heat (without using any fan-forced function) for at least 20 minutes (see page 89). Thinly slice the mozzarella and scatter evenly, here and there, to top the shaped pizza base, leaving the edges clear to about 3–4 cm (1½ inches). Arrange the salame 'straws' on top and sprinkle over the grated parmesan. Place the pizza in the oven for 3–5 minutes until cooked, turning to get an even colour. Once out of the oven, arrange the chopped chicory over the pizza. Dollop the stracciatella on top and distribute the confit tomatoes over the lot. Drizzle with olive oil and add the pepper.

Makes one 30 cm (12 inch) pizza

Pancetta, wilted rucola and taleggio

Taleggio is a washed-rind, soft cheese with a strong flavour from Italy's Lombardy region. It tones down somewhat on cooking, but the smellier, the better. I love using rocket as a cooked ingredient rather than just as a salad leaf. Here it adds colour as well as a spicy note.

INGREDIENTS

250 g (9 oz) ball of basic pizza dough
  (see pages 74–77), shaped
  (see pages 80–83)

100 g (3½ oz/3 cups) rocket (arugula),
  thick stems removed
100 g (3½ oz) fior di latte mozzarella
1 tablespoon grated parmesan cheese
100 g (3½ oz) taleggio cheese, cut into
  small cubes
A couple of pinches of freshly ground
  black pepper
12 slices of good-quality pancetta
1 tablespoon extra virgin olive oil

METHOD

TO ASSEMBLE / Place a large tile in your oven for the pizza, then preheat to full heat (without using any fan-forced function) for at least 20 minutes (see page 89). Bring a pot of salted water to the boil. Plunge in the rocket leaves, submerging them using a wooden spoon. Blanch for 2 minutes, drain and let cool before squeezing well to expel most of the water and roughly chopping.

Thinly slice the mozzarella and scatter evenly, here and there, to top the shaped pizza base, leaving the edges clear to about 3–4 cm (1½ inches). Arrange the cooked, chopped rocket on the mozzarella and sprinkle the parmesan over the lot. Place the pizza in the oven for 3–5 minutes until cooked, turning to get an even colour. Once out of the oven, arrange the taleggio on top, sprinkle with pepper, drape the pancetta over and drizzle with the olive oil.

Makes one 30 cm (12 inch) pizza

THIS PAGE / Picturesque streets of the small fishing village of Cetara.

Gorgonzola, potato and radicchio

Most often it's the soft, delicate cheeses that are used on pizza, but when an assertive blue like gorgonzola is used, it dominates. The other ingredients support and complement. Potato is there for texture, radicchio as a flavour foil and rosemary binds the whole.

INGREDIENTS

250 g (9 oz) ball of basic pizza dough
   (see pages 74–77), shaped
   (see pages 80–83)

100 g (3½ oz) fior di latte mozzarella
40 g (1½ oz/1 cup) radicchio leaves,
   sliced in 2 cm (¾ inch) wide strips
80 g (3 oz) gorgonzola cheese, cut into
   12 pieces
12 very thin slices of potato (see note)
A pinch of sea salt
Freshly ground black pepper
1 teaspoon fresh young rosemary leaves

ROSEMARY OIL

2 tablespoons fresh young rosemary leaves
170 ml (5½ fl oz/⅔ cup) extra virgin
   olive oil

METHOD

FOR THE ROSEMARY OIL / Finely chop the rosemary leaves with a very sharp knife. Place in a bowl and cover the leaves with the olive oil. Cover the bowl and place in a cool spot for 2 hours. Remove the leaves from the oil by passing through a fine sieve. Place the oil in a small squeezy bottle, ready to use. Any leftover oil can be kept in the refrigerator for up to a month.

TO ASSEMBLE / Place a large tile in your oven for the pizza, then turn the oven up to preheat to full heat (without using any fan-forced function) for at least 20 minutes (see page 89). Thinly slice the mozzarella and scatter evenly, here and there, to top the shaped pizza base, leaving the edges clear to about 3–4 cm (1½ inches). Scatter the radicchio and gorgonzola evenly over the pizza. Lay the potato slices on top. Season with a little salt, a couple of turns of the pepper mill and cook the pizza for 3–5 minutes until cooked, turning to get an even colour. Once out of the oven, drizzle with 1 tablespoon of the rosemary oil, scatter the rosemary leaves on top and serve.

Makes one 30 cm (12 inch) pizza

NOTE Use waxy, yellow-fleshed potatoes and to cut them very thin, use a mandolin or a food processor with a potato slicer. It's important that the potato slices are thin and see-through because they have to cook in a relatively short amount of time.

Montasio, broccoli and prosciutto crackle

Montasio is a firm, flavoursome mountain cheese from the regions of Friuli and Veneto in northeastern Italy. When it melts, it adds a little bite to the broccoli cream. The fried prosciutto is added as a final crisp and salty note.

INGREDIENTS

250 g (9 oz) ball of basic pizza dough
    (see pages 74–77), shaped
    (see pages 80–83)

3 large asparagus spears
80 g (3 oz) fior di latte mozzarella
1 tablespoon extra virgin olive oil
A pinch of sea salt
Freshly ground black pepper
60 g (2 oz) Montasio cheese, shaved
    using a potato peeler

PROSCIUTTO CRACKLE
80 ml (2½ fl oz/⅓ cup) extra virgin
    olive oil
8 thin slices of prosciutto

BROCCOLI CREAM
200 g (7 oz/3 cups) broccoli florets
3 tablespoons extra virgin olive oil
2–3 pinches of sea salt
A pinch of white pepper

METHOD

FOR THE PROSCIUTTO CRACKLE / Place the olive oil in a pan as wide as a slice of prosciutto. Place over a medium–high heat. When the oil is hot, lay the slices in, making sure they are not overlapping. It may mean frying only two or three at a time, depending on the slices and the pan size. After a minute or so, turn each rasher using tongs. When crisp, remove and put on a plate with paper towel. To store any extra, place on paper towel in a sealed plastic container in a cool place. Don't store in the refrigerator.

FOR THE BROCCOLI CREAM / Blanch the broccoli florets in boiling water for 2 minutes and then drain well. Using a stick blender or food processor, blend with the olive oil, salt and pepper until smooth. Cool before using. Fill a piping bag with 4 tablespoons of the broccoli cream. Any left-over cream can be kept in the refrigerator for up to 5 days.

TO ASSEMBLE / Place a large tile in your oven for the pizza, then turn the oven up to preheat to full heat (without using any fan-forced function) for at least 20 minutes (see page 89). Blanch the asparagus in boiling water for 20 seconds. Slice each asparagus spear in half, top to bottom.

Thinly slice the mozzarella and scatter evenly, here and there, to top the shaped pizza base, leaving the edges clear to about 3–4 cm (1½ inches). Arrange each asparagus half evenly on the mozzarella. Drizzle with the olive oil. Season with a little salt, a couple of turns of the pepper mill and place the pizza in the oven for 3–5 minutes until cooked, turning to get an even colour. Once out of the oven, scatter with the shaved Montasio and crush one or two rashers of the prosciutto crackle over the top. Pipe small blobs of the broccoli cream here and there to finish.

Makes one 30 cm (12 inch) pizza

Prosciutto and bufala

This has become a modern classic with many pizzerie offering their own version. Once again, it's the quality of the ingredients that set the best apart. My preference is for 24 month-aged Prosciutto di Parma. The prosciutto is always best sliced at the last minute.

INGREDIENTS

250 g (9 oz) ball of basic pizza dough
    (see pages 74–77), shaped
    (see pages 80–83)

120 g (4¼ oz) buffalo mozzarella
1 tablespoon grated parmesan cheese
35 g (1¼ oz/1 cup) rocket (arugula), thick
    stems removed
6–8 slices of Prosciutto di Parma
1 tablespoon extra virgin olive oil

ROAST CHERRY TOMATOES

1 kg (2 lb 4 oz) cherry or small roma
    (plum) tomatoes
2 tablespoons extra virgin olive oil
Sea salt and freshly ground black pepper

METHOD

FOR THE ROAST CHERRY TOMATOES / Preheat the oven to 170°C (340°F). Prepare the tomatoes by slicing them in half and place, cut side up, on a baking tray. Drizzle with the olive oil, salt and pepper and roast for about 15 minutes. Remove and let them cool before using. Any leftover tomatoes can be kept in the refrigerator for up to 5 days.

TO ASSEMBLE / Place a large tile in your oven for the pizza, then turn the oven up to preheat to full heat (without using any fan-forced function) for at least 20 minutes (see page 89). Cut the mozzarella into 1 cm (½ inch) cubes and scatter evenly, here and there, to top the shaped pizza base, leaving the edges clear to about 3–4 cm (1½ inches). Scatter the parmesan on top and then evenly distribute 18 of the roast cherry tomato halves over the top. Place the pizza in the oven for 3–5 minutes until cooked, turning to get an even colour. Once out, scatter the rocket leaves over, arrange the prosciutto slices evenly and drizzle with olive oil.

Makes one 30 cm (12 inch) pizza

Pumpkin, scamorza and zucchini flowers

This is another flavour from my childhood and recalls my mother's pumpkin tortelli. The pumpkin type is important. Butternut pumpkins (squash) are not flavoursome enough. Traditionally Mantovane pumpkins are used, but I've had success with Japanese and Australian Queensland Blue pumpkins too. Try to avoid just-picked pumpkins: they need to age a little so they lose some moisture.

INGREDIENTS

250 g (9 oz) ball of basic pizza dough
    (see pages 74–77), shaped
    (see pages 80–83)

120 g (4¼ oz/½ cup) ricotta cheese
2 tablespoons grated parmesan cheese
8 thin slices of smoked scamorza cheese
3 female zucchini (courgette) flowers,
    zucchini attached
1 tablespoon toasted pine nuts
Sea salt and freshly ground black pepper
12 Gaeta (or similar) black olives, pitted
1 tablespoon extra virgin olive oil

PUMPKIN PUREE

1 pumpkin (winter squash), weighing
    roughly 2.5 kg (5 lb 8 oz)
100 g (3½ oz) unsalted butter
1 large onion, cut into 1 cm (½ inch) cubes
2 garlic cloves, crushed
80 g (3 oz) amaretti biscuits, crushed
100 g (3½ oz/1 cup) grated Grana
    Padano cheese
120 g (4¼ oz) mustard fruit – apple, pear
    or quince, finely chopped
2 good pinches of ground nutmeg
Sea salt and freshly ground black pepper

METHOD

FOR THE PUMPKIN PUREE / Cut the pumpkin into pieces of the same size. Remove the pips and soft webbing around them, but don't remove the skin. Put the pumpkin in a steamer and steam for 15–20 minutes until cooked, soft and tender. A sharp knife should easily pierce the flesh all the way through. Drain and leave to cool a little. Use a fork to scrape the flesh off the skin, not a spoon. Sometimes a pumpkin has woody pieces and with a fork you can feel these. Scoop the flesh off the skin and into a bowl, scraping even the green part near the skin – it's the best part so try to get as much of that as possible. Put the pumpkin flesh, in small amounts at a time, into a clean dish towel and squeeze out as much of the liquid as possible. Heat the butter in a pan and lightly fry the onion until it begins to colour. Take off the heat and strain off the butter, keeping it aside to cool. Discard the onion. Add the cooled butter and crushed garlic to the pumpkin. Mix in the crushed amaretti, Grana Padano, chopped mustard fruit and nutmeg. Season to taste. Any left-over purée will keep for up to 5 days in the refrigerator.

TO ASSEMBLE / Place a large tile in your oven for the pizza, then turn the oven up to preheat to full heat (without using any fan-forced function) for at least 20 minutes (see page 89). Mix together the ricotta and parmesan cheeses and place into a piping bag. Cut each slice of scamorza in half, giving 16 pieces. Remove the flowers from the zucchini and cut each flower in half. Slice the zucchini into thin rounds. Spread 6 tablespoons of the pumpkin purée carefully on top of the shaped pizza base, leaving the edges clear to about 3–4 cm (1½ inches). Distribute the scamorza on top and then evenly scatter over the zucchini slices and the pine nuts. Sprinkle on a pinch or two of salt and pepper and place the pizza in the oven for 3–5 minutes until cooked, turning to get an even colour. Once out of the oven, scatter the zucchini flowers, cut side up, on top and pipe into each some ricotta mixture. Also pipe some ricotta around the pizza. Finish with the olives and drizzle with the olive oil.

Makes one 30 cm (12 inch) pizza

Lucariello, onion confettura and burrata

Lucariello are a variety of tomatoes grown in the Sarnese-Nocerino zone of Campania, which also produces San Marzano DOP, the tomatoes of choice for traditional pizzaioli. They are small, yellow, pear-shaped tomatoes with a thick skin and firm flesh. Their subtle flavour is used to accompany delicate ingredients on pizze. Lucariello are produced only by a handful of growers and all the production is snapped up each year by eager pizzaioli. If not available, use small yellow tomatoes.

INGREDIENTS

250 g (9 oz) ball of basic pizza dough
(see pages 74–77), shaped
(see pages 80–83)

6 lucariello tomatoes, each cut in half
Sea salt
80 g (3 oz) burrata, cut into 8–10 pieces
2 tablespoons fresh tarragon leaves
1 tablespoon extra virgin olive oil

ONION CONFETTURA

3 tablespoons extra virgin olive oil
2 kg (4lb 8 oz) sweet white onions, thinly
sliced
1 teaspoon sea salt
1 teaspoon freshly ground black pepper
300 ml (10½ fl oz) vegetable stock
3 tablespoons white wine vinegar

METHOD

FOR THE ONION CONFETTURA / Heat the olive oil in a large heavy-based frying pan with high sides and add the onion, salt and pepper. Reduce the heat to medium–low and simmer, occasionally stirring, for about 30–40 minutes until the onion is very soft but not coloured. Add the vegetable stock and vinegar. Keep simmering until the pan is dry and the onion is golden – about 30–40 minutes or more depending on the heat. Correct the seasoning by adding a little more salt if necessary and stir well. Any extra keeps for weeks in the fridge, but remove and bring to room temperature before use.

TO ASSEMBLE / Place a large tile in your oven for the pizza, then turn the oven up to preheat to full heat (without using any fan-forced function) for at least 20 minutes (see page 89). Spread 4 tablespoons of the onion confettura onto the shaped pizza base, leaving the edges clear to about 3–4 cm (1½ inches). Scatter the tomatoes on top and then season with a couple of pinches of salt. Place the pizza in the oven for 3–5 minutes until cooked, turning to get an even colour. Once ready, remove from the oven and scatter the burrata on top, immediately followed by the tarragon leaves. Drizzle with the olive oil.

Makes one 30 cm (12 inch) pizza

Beetroot, onion and roast garlic

This is a combination from my childhood. My mother would cook up a simple 'bollito' of beetroot and onion and dress it with good olive oil, parsley and garlic. We would eat it with bread. Here the pizza base takes the place of bread. Use a mix of red and yellow beetroot (beets) if available.

INGREDIENTS

250 g (9 oz) ball of basic pizza dough
    (see pages 74–77), shaped
    (see pages 80–83)

100 g (3½ oz) fior di latte mozzarella
1 tablespoon grated pecorino cheese
1 tablespoon chopped fresh parsley

COOKED BEETROOT AND ONIONS
6 medium–large beetroot (beets), tops off,
    skin left on
8 onions, skin left on

ROAST GARLIC DRESSING
4 garlic bulbs (heads), left whole
200 ml (7 fl oz) extra virgin
    olive oil
6 anchovies, chopped into small pieces
Sea salt and freshly ground black pepper

METHOD

FOR THE COOKED BEETROOT AND ONIONS / In a large pot, cover the beetroot and onions with cold water and bring to the boil. Turn the heat down to a simmer and cook for about 12–15 minutes until the vegetables are cooked. Peel the beetroot, cut each into eight wedges and place in a bowl. Squeeze out the middles of the onions and discard the tough skin. Cut each onion into four and place in a bowl. Any left-over beetroot and onion will keep for up to a week in the refrigerator.

FOR THE ROAST GARLIC DRESSING / Preheat the oven to 140°C (275°F). Roast the whole garlic bulbs on a tray for 30 minutes until they are soft. Cut the bulbs in half and squeeze the garlic out like toothpaste into a bowl. Mash with a fork, add the olive oil and the anchovies, season and mix thoroughly. Any left-over dressing will keep for up to a week in the refrigerator.

TO ASSEMBLE / Place a large tile in your oven for the pizza, then turn the oven up to preheat to full heat (without using any fan-forced function) for at least 20 minutes (see page 89). Thinly slice the mozzarella and scatter evenly, here and there, to top the shaped pizza base, leaving the edges clear to about 3–4 cm (1½ inches). Arrange eight wedges of cooked onion and twelve beetroot wedges on the mozzarella and sprinkle the pecorino over the lot. Place the pizza in the oven for 3–5 minutes until cooked, turning to get an even colour. Once out of the oven, drizzle with 1 tablespoon of the roast garlic dressing and sprinkle the parsley on top.

Makes one 30 cm (12 inch) pizza

THIS PAGE / Streets of Altamura in Puglia.

Quattro formaggi and walnuts

Here's another take on a modern classic – the four cheeses. You could make it five by adding a final sprinkling of grated Parmigiano. I've added walnuts and quite a bit of pepper.

INGREDIENTS

250 g (9 oz) ball of basic pizza dough
  (see pages 74–77), shaped
  (see pages 80–83)

120 g (4¼ oz) fior di latte mozzarella
80 g (3 oz/⅓ cup) ricotta cheese
80 g (3 oz) gorgonzola cheese, cut into
  1 cm (½ inch) cubes
100 g (3½ oz/1 cup) grated pecorino
  cheese
120 g (4¼ oz/1 cup) fresh, shelled walnut
  pieces
½ teaspoon freshly ground black pepper

METHOD

TO ASSEMBLE / Place a large tile in your oven for the pizza, then turn the oven up to preheat to full heat (without using any fan-forced function) for at least 20 minutes (see page 89). Thinly slice the mozzarella and scatter evenly, here and there, to top the shaped pizza base, leaving the edges clear to about 3–4 cm (1½ inches). Spoon the ricotta in blobs over the mozzarella and place the gorgonzola cubes randomly in places where there is no ricotta. Scatter pecorino evenly over the lot and distribute the walnut pieces throughout. Finally, season with the black pepper and place the pizza in the oven for 3–5 minutes until cooked, turning to get an even colour.

Makes one 30 cm (12 inch) pizza

Pork and fennel sausage, artichoke, buffalo ricotta

I've taken the filling out of the sausage casings for good reason. If the sausage is merely sliced, the casings can have the texture of rubber bands when cooked quickly at high heat. It's also easier to distribute the sausage evenly on the pizza. If fresh artichokes aren't available, there are good Italian artichokes in oil available at specialist stores.

INGREDIENTS

250 g (9 oz) ball of basic pizza dough (see pages 74–77), shaped (see pages 80–83)

120 g (4¼ oz) fior di latte mozzarella, thinly sliced
3 cooked artichokes (see note), cut into quarters
40 g (1½ oz/¾ cup) grated parmesan cheese
140 g (5 oz) best-quality Italian-style pork and fennel sausages, meat removed from casings
Sea salt
80 g (3 oz/⅓ cup) buffalo milk ricotta cheese
8–10 fennel fronds

TOMATO FILLETS
1 kg (2 lb 4 oz) ripe tomatoes
Sea salt

METHOD

FOR THE TOMATO FILLETS / Plunge the tomatoes into boiling salted water for 20–30 seconds, then plunge into iced water. After 5 minutes, they'll peel easily. Peel, halve and scoop out all seeds with a spoon. Cut each half in two, then each quarter into fillets. Unused fillets will keep for 2–3 days, refrigerated.

TO ASSEMBLE / Place a large tile in your oven for the pizza, then turn the oven up to preheat to full heat (without using any fan-forced function) for at least 20 minutes (see page 89). Scatter mozzarella over the pizza base, leaving the edges clear to about 3–4 cm (1½ inches). Distribute the artichoke quarters and tomato fillets over the top. Sprinkle with parmesan and sausage meat. Season with salt and place in the oven for 3–5 minutes until cooked, turning for even colour. Once out of the oven, use a teaspoon to place small blobs of buffalo ricotta here and there. Finally, place the fennel fronds evenly over the top.

Makes one 30 cm (12 inch) pizza

NOTE / Choose artichokes that are firm, without blemishes and have heads that are full and tight. To prepare you'll need a pan of cold water with the juice of a lemon squeezed into it to prevent discolouring. With a paring knife, take the top 2–3 cm (1 inch) of the artichoke clean off, then begin paring around the heart until you reach the tender inner leaves. Leave about 4–5 cm (2 inches) of stalk at the base, this part being quite delicious when cooked, and trim away any leaves. As each artichoke is prepared, place it in the pan of lemon water. You will notice that the artichokes float and the topmost ones sit above the water – weight down with a plate so they don't discolour. Bring the water to the boil, turn down to a simmer and cook for 10–15 minutes until tender. Test for 'doneness' by pushing a knife into one of the artichokes – there should be just a hint of resistance. Drain and cool the artichokes completely. Any tough outer leaves can be removed and the stem trimmed. Store the artichokes in jars under olive oil for up to 14 days in the refrigerator or slice or quarter and use within 3–4 days.

THIS PAGE / Red poppies among the olive trees in the Alta Murgia, Puglia.

Lamb belly, ricotta and Mediterranean herbs

This pizza has become somewhat of a Pizzaperta signature. We put it on the menu when lamb is at its best, approaching spring and early summer. It can be done exactly the same way using kid goat or pork belly. A typical lamb belly will weigh between 600–800 g (1 lb 5 oz–1 lb 12 oz). It will shrink slightly once cooked, but if you choose two bellies within these weight parameters, there should be enough to make six or more pizze.

INGREDIENTS

250 g (9 oz) ball of basic pizza dough
    (see pages 74–77), shaped
    (see pages 80–83)

80 g (3 oz/⅓ cup) ricotta cheese
40 g (1½ oz/½ cup) grated parmesan
    cheese
100 g (3½ oz) fior di latte mozzarella
6 tomato fillets (see page 142)
Sea salt and freshly ground black pepper
1 tablespoon Mediterranean herbs –
    rosemary, sage, thyme, oregano and
    marjoram, finely chopped

SLOW-COOKED LAMB BELLY

1.2 kg (2 lb 10 oz) lamb belly, trimmed of
    any excess fat
1 carrot, cut into 1 cm (½ inch) rounds
1 celery stalk, cut into 1 cm (½ inch) slices
2 garlic cloves, peeled and left whole
1 small onion, chopped
2 bay leaves
8 peppercorns
1–2 litres (35–70 fl oz/4–8 cups) lamb or
    chicken stock

METHOD

FOR THE SLOW-COOKED LAMB BELLY / Preheat the oven to 140°C (275°F). Place the lamb bellies side by side, not overlapping, in an oven dish. Place all the vegetables, bay leaves and peppercorns around. Pour in the stock and make sure the meat is covered by at least 1 cm (½ inch) of liquid. If not, just increase the amount of stock. Cover the dish tightly with foil and place in the oven for 4 hours. After this time, check to see if it's cooked. If a sharp skewer pierces the meat easily, it is done. If not, leave it in longer. Once cooked, remove the meat from the liquid and let it cool. Drain the vegetables from the liquid and place the cooled stock in the refrigerator. Once solid, remove any fat from the surface and it can be reused (it can also be frozen). Place the cool lamb belly on a dish and place a weight on top. Keep in the refrigerator overnight. The weight will keep the lamb belly uniform in thickness. It is now ready to use. Any left-over lamb belly will keep for up to 5 days, refrigerated.

TO ASSEMBLE / Place a large tile in your oven for the pizza, then turn the oven up to preheat to full heat (without using any fan-forced function) for at least 20 minutes (see page 89). Cut about a sixth of the lamb into 12 thin rectangles. Mix the ricotta and parmesan together and place in a small piping bag. Thinly slice the mozzarella and scatter evenly, here and there, to top the shaped pizza base, leaving the edges clear to about 3–4 cm (1½ inches). Place the tomato fillets across the top. Distribute the lamb pieces evenly on the pizza and season. Place the pizza into the oven for 3–5 minutes until cooked, turning to get an even colour. Once out of the oven, pipe the ricotta and parmesan mixture in small blobs over the cooked pizza and sprinkle with the chopped herbs.

Makes one 30 cm (12 inch) pizza

Black truffle and fontina

We make this pizza during the winter black truffle season. The only thing that's better to use is fresh white truffle. Use a purpose-made truffle shaver to thinly slice the truffle and cover the pizza. Fontina is a cow's milk washed-rind cheese from the northwestern Italian alpine region of Valle d'Aosta.

INGREDIENTS

250 g (9 oz) ball of basic pizza dough
    (see pages 74–77), shaped
    (see pages 80–83)

120 g (4¼ oz) fontina cheese
50 g (2 oz/½ cup) grated
    parmesan cheese
Sea salt and freshly ground black pepper
5–10 g (⅛–¼ oz) fresh black truffle

METHOD

TO ASSEMBLE / Place a large tile in your oven for the pizza, then turn the oven up to preheat to full heat (without using any fan-forced function) for at least 20 minutes (see page 89). Thinly slice the fontina and scatter evenly, here and there, to top the shaped pizza base, leaving the edges clear to about 3–4 cm (1½ inches). Sprinkle the parmesan evenly over the lot. Finally, season with a couple of pinches of salt and freshly ground pepper and place the pizza into the oven for 3–5 minutes until cooked, turning to get an even colour. Once out of the oven, shave the black truffle immediately on the pizza as the heat will release the truffle's aroma. Serve straightaway.

Makes one 30 cm (12 inch) pizza

Capocollo, pickled red onion and pecorino

Capocollo is cured pork neck. Use a semi-hard pecorino cheese, rather than a firm, grating style. The pickled red onion recipe makes enough for 6 pizze. Any extra can be served as an accompaniment to grilled meats or seafood or used as an addition to summer salads.

INGREDIENTS

250 g (9 oz) ball of basic pizza dough
(see pages 74–77), shaped
(see pages 80–83)

100 g (3½ oz) fior di latte mozzarella
12 thin slices of capocollo di Martina
Franca
60 g (2 oz/¾ cup) pecorino cheese
shavings
Freshly ground black pepper

PICKLED RED ONION
4 large red onions, halved and thinly sliced
250 ml (9 fl oz/1 cup) red wine vinegar
50 g (2 oz/¼ cup) sugar
125 ml (4 fl oz/½ cup) water
2 tablespoons extra virgin olive oil
1 tablespoon finely chopped fresh parsley
Sea salt and freshly ground black pepper

METHOD

FOR THE PICKLED RED ONION / Place the sliced onion in a wide, shallow, preferably ceramic dish. Bring the vinegar, sugar and water to the boil in a saucepan and immediately pour the boiling liquid onto the onion. Let cool to room temperature. The onion is now ready to be drained and used or stored in its liquid – it will become tastier over a few days. To serve, drain and squeeze out the vinegar, dress with extra virgin olive oil and the parsley and season. Pickled onions can be stored in their liquid, in the refrigerator, for up to a month.

TO ASSEMBLE / Place a large tile in your oven for the pizza, then turn the oven up to preheat to full heat (without using any fan-forced function) for at least 20 minutes (see page 89). Thinly slice the mozzarella and scatter evenly, here and there, to top the shaped pizza base, leaving the edges clear to about 3–4 cm (1½ inches). Place the pizza in the oven for 3–5 minutes until cooked, turning to get an even colour. Once cooked, place the capocollo slices over the cooked pizza and scatter the shaved pecorino on top with a few grinds of black pepper. Finally, scatter 3 tablespoons of the pickled red onion over the top.

Makes one 30 cm (12 inch) pizza

Pickled lettuce, capers, olives and tomatoes

This is an unusual topping for pizza. If good-quality vinegar is used when pickling the lettuce and the leaves are squeezed to expel all the liquid before using on the pizza, then the result is excellent. I use small date tomatoes because they tend to be super sweet with little acid, counteracting the pickle.

INGREDIENTS

250 g (9 oz) ball of basic pizza dough
   (see pages 74–77), shaped
   (see pages 80–83)

100 g (3½ oz) fior di latte mozzarella
40 g (1½ oz/¾ cup) grated parmesan
   cheese
12 Gaeta (or similar) black olives, pitted
2 tablespoons Sicilian capers, soaked and
   desalted (see page 36)
Freshly ground black pepper

CONFIT TOMATOES
1 kg (2 lb 4 oz) ripe date, cherry or any
   small tomatoes
6 garlic cloves, halved
3–4 sprigs of fresh thyme or any other
   herbs
Sea salt and freshly ground black pepper
150 ml (5 fl oz) extra virgin olive oil

PICKLED LETTUCE
500 g (1 lb 2 oz) lettuce leaves, various
   types
3 garlic cloves, halved
1 tablespoon red or white wine vinegar
2 tablespoons extra virgin olive oil
Sea salt and freshly ground black pepper

METHOD

FOR THE CONFIT TOMATOES / Preheat the oven to 140°C (275°F). Cut the tomatoes in half, top to bottom. Place in an oven dish so that the tomatoes fill the bottom of the dish in one layer. Add the garlic and thyme. Season with three to four good pinches of salt and three to four turns of freshly ground pepper. Add the olive oil and mix everything carefully with a spoon. Place in the oven for 30–40 minutes. The tomatoes are ready when they're soft but not falling apart. Any extra tomatoes can be cooled and stored in the refrigerator, in a covered container, with all their cooking juices, for up to 10 days.

FOR THE PICKLED LETTUCE / Prepare the lettuce leaves by discarding any brown ones and trimming any tough roots or stalks. Place in a large sink and wash well to remove any sand or grit. Bring a large pot of water to the boil. Add the lettuce and blanch for 2 minutes. Drain well and place the leaves in a large bowl with the garlic cloves, vinegar and extra virgin olive oil. Season to taste with salt and pepper and toss well. Make sure the lettuce is squeezed well, expelling as much liquid as possible, before using on pizza. Any left-over lettuce will keep for up to 3 days, refrigerated.

TO ASSEMBLE / Place a large tile in your oven for the pizza, then turn the oven up to preheat to full heat (without using any fan-forced function) for at least 20 minutes (see page 89). Thinly slice the mozzarella and scatter evenly, here and there, to top the shaped pizza base, leaving the edges clear to about 3–4 cm (1½ inches). Sprinkle with the parmesan. Evenly distribute six to eight leaves of the pickled lettuce, the olives, capers and eighteen well-drained confit tomato halves on top. Place the pizza in the oven for 3–5 minutes until cooked, turning to get an even colour. Once cooked, finish with a couple of turns of the pepper mill and serve immediately.

Makes one 30 cm (12 inch) pizza

LANZA

(PRECOOKED)

These next two chapters use the Roman-style pizza dough to produce a very different style pizza to the Neapolitan. More closely related to the focaccia tradition, the pizze are cooked at lower temperatures in a conventional oven rather than a wood-fired one.

I have called this first chapter 'precooked'. The dough is cooked, allowed to cool, and then cut into squares or tiles before reheating and topping or filling. The great thing about the Roman-style pizza dough is that once cooked, it can be covered and stored in the refrigerator for 4–5 days before using. The following chapter I call 'predressed' because the dough is dressed with some or all of the ingredients before it is cooked.

You'll notice I use the word 'teglia' occasionally. It means the sheet of dough as well as referring to the tray that the dough has been cooked in.

Roman pizza with prosciutto, burrata and eggplant

I first had this combination at Antonio Pappalardo's Cascina dei Sapori in Rezzato, Brescia. I fell in love with the richness of the burrata and the salty goodness of the prosciutto. Above all, I loved the base – soft and airy inside and crisp on the outside

INGREDIENTS

1 sheet of Roman-style pizza dough
   (see pages 84–88), precooked
   (see page 89) and cut into 8 squares

8 thin slices of hot chargrilled eggplant
   (aubergine) (see page 98)
8 thin slices of Prosciutto di Parma or similar
1 or 2 burrata, depending on size, cut into
   8 in a bowl
Sea salt and freshly ground black pepper

METHOD

TO ASSEMBLE / Place the Roman pizza squares on a baking tray and heat in a preheated 180°C (350°F) oven for 5–6 minutes until they are crisp on the outside but soft in the middle. Once ready, remove from the oven. Form a cup using a piece of hot chargrilled eggplant in the middle and a slice of prosciutto on the outside. Place this neatly on each square and arrange on plates. Spoon the burrata into the middle of the cup. The burrata will fall apart because it is soft, but can be handled using a tablespoon. Season lightly with salt and freshly ground pepper.

Makes 8 squares

Roman pizza with figs, prosciutto and balsamic

There is way too much balsamic vinegar used these days. And most of it is that poor supermarket-bought tangy brown liquid sweetened with caramel. If you're going to use balsamic in this classic combination, spend a little more on the good stuff. It's well worth it.

INGREDIENTS

1 sheet of Roman-style pizza dough
(see pages 84–88), precooked
(see page 89) and cut into 8 squares

8 ripe figs, sliced into 5 mm (¼ inch) rounds
16 thin slices of Prosciutto di Parma
or similar
2 teaspoons aged balsamic vinegar
Sea salt and freshly ground black pepper

METHOD

TO ASSEMBLE / Cut each pizza square in half, opening it to form a 'sandwich'. Place the halves back together on a baking tray and heat in a preheated 180°C (350°F) oven for 5–6 minutes until they are crisp on the outside but soft in the middle. Once ready, remove from the oven. Place the bottoms of each square on the work surface and lay the slices of fig down first. Next, add two slices of prosciutto per square. Finally, sprinkle with the balsamic, season lightly with salt and freshly ground pepper and place the top half of the square on each.

Makes 8 filled Roman pizze

Roman pizza with octopus and potato

Choose a yellow-fleshed potato such as Nicola or Spunta and cook in their jackets until tender. Taggiasche olives are small dark-green to black olives from Liguria. They have a distinctive flavour. If unavailable, use another green or black olive. Your fishmonger will clean the octopus by removing the innards from the head and the 'beak'. The cooking time will depend on the species as well as the thickness of the octopus's tentacles.

INGREDIENTS

1 sheet of Roman-style pizza dough
    (see pages 84–88), precooked
    (see page 89) and cut into 8 squares

3 tablespoons extra virgin olive oil
Sea salt
400 g (14 oz) cooked potatoes, peeled

SLOW-COOKED OCTOPUS

1.2 kg (2 lb 10 oz) octopus, cleaned
    and washed
Sea salt
1 onion, quartered
1 celery stalk, cut into 2 cm (¾ inch) lengths
1 carrot, cut into 2 cm (¾ inch) lengths
2 bay leaves
10–12 fresh parsley stalks

CAPER AND OLIVE DRESSING

2 tablespoons extra virgin olive oil
50 g (2 oz/⅓ cup) Sicilian capers, soaked
    and desalted (see page 36), roughly
    chopped
60 g (2 oz/½ cup) pitted Taggiasche
    olives, roughly chopped
1 tablespoon finely chopped fresh parsley
Juice of 1 lemon
Sea salt and freshly ground black pepper

METHOD

FOR THE SLOW-COOKED OCTOPUS / Start with a large pot of cold water so the octopus is completely immersed a good 10 cm (4 inches) below the top of the water level. Add two to three pinches of salt, the onion, celery, carrot, bay leaves and parsley stalks. Bring to the boil, turn down to a simmer and cook for 40–60 minutes, until tender. Let the octopus cool down in its cooking liquid. Once cooled, cut it into bite-sized pieces to fit on your pizza.

FOR THE CAPER AND OLIVE DRESSING / Mix all the ingredients together in a bowl and season with salt and pepper, to taste. Any left-over dressing can be stored for up to 10 days in the refrigerator.

TO ASSEMBLE / Place the Roman pizza squares on a baking tray and heat in a preheated 180°C (350°F) oven for about 5–6 minutes until they are crisp on the outside but soft in the middle. Meanwhile, make sure all the other ingredients are ready. While the pizza is in the oven, pat dry the octopus and cook on a chargrill pan or in a frying pan in a little olive oil until well coloured. Season and set aside. Once ready, remove the pizza squares from the oven and, using a ricer, mash the cooked potato directly and evenly over the tiles. Use a fork to help spread the potato. Arrange the grilled octopus pieces on top of the pizza. Finally, spoon 6 tablespoons of the caper and olive dressing on top.

Makes 8 squares

Roman pizza with roast duck, chestnuts and mushrooms

Ideally this is an autumn pizza, when chestnuts and mushrooms, both wild and cultivated, are plentiful and in season. However, use whatever mushrooms are available.

INGREDIENTS

1 sheet of Roman-style pizza dough
   (see pages 84–88), precooked
   (see page 89) and cut into 8 squares

CHESTNUT PUREE
500 g (1 lb 2 oz) chestnuts
8 whole peppercorns
Rind from ½ orange (in 4–5 large peels)
1 tablespoon extra virgin olive oil
Sea salt

ROAST DUCK BREAST
4 duck breasts
2 pinches of sea salt

BRAISED MUSHROOMS
1 leek, washed thoroughly and sliced
2 garlic cloves, crushed
2 tablespoons extra virgin olive oil
500 g (1 lb 2 oz) assorted fresh
   mushrooms, such as buttons, shiitake,
   chestnut and fresh porcini, sliced
A large handful of finely chopped
   fresh parsley
Sea salt and freshly ground black pepper

METHOD

FOT THE CHESTNUT PUREE / Score the chestnuts by cutting a shallow cross on the flat sides with the tip of a sharp knife. Place in boiling water with the peppercorns and orange rind for 15 minutes. They must be tender – test by piercing one with the tip of the knife. Once cooked, drain (keeping a cup of the cooking liquid) and peel as soon as they're cool enough to handle. They'll peel better when still warm, but do make sure both skin and fine inner pellicle are removed. Press the chestnut flesh through a ricer like you would potatoes for gnocchi. Add the olive oil and enough of the reserved cooking liquid to soften the purée. Blend with a stick blender until smooth. Add a little more cooking liquid if necessary so the purée is smooth and creamy. Season and gently heat in a small pan just before using. Any extra can be refrigerated for up to 1 week.

FOR THE ROAST DUCK BREAST / Preheat the oven to 220°C (425°F). Sprinkle the duck skin with salt. Heat a heavy-based frying pan and fry the breasts skin-side down over a medium flame for a few minutes. This will crisp the skin as well as removing most of the fat. Discard the fat and, keeping the duck pieces skin side down in the pan, place in the oven. The breast will take about 6–8 minutes, depending on size. Rest for 5 minutes, then slice into thin pieces. Any left-over duck can be stored in the refrigerator for up to 2 days.

FOR THE BRAISED MUSHROOMS / Place the leek and garlic in a wide braising pan with the oil and fry gently to soften, but don't colour. Turn up the heat and immediately add the mushrooms. Stir continuously for 2–3 minutes until soft. Lower the heat, simmer for 10 minutes, then mix in the parsley and season. Drain any liquid, keeping it in a small bowl.

TO ASSEMBLE / Place the Roman pizza squares on a baking tray and heat in a preheated 180°C (350°F) oven for about 5–6 minutes until they are crisp on the outside but soft in the middle. Once ready, remove from the oven. Spread the warm chestnut purée on the tiles, arrange the duck on top and finish with the mushrooms. Finally, spoon a little of the mushroom cooking liquid on top.

Makes 8 squares

Roman pizza with grilled ox tongue, parsnip purée, salsa verde

Ox tongue with salsa verde is a dish from my family roots in Brescia. It makes a delicious winter pizza with the addition of parsnip purée.

INGREDIENTS

1 sheet of Roman-style pizza dough
  (see pages 84–88), precooked
  (see page 89) and cut into 8 squares

GRILLED OX TONGUE WITH SALSA VERDE

1 ox (beef) tongue, about 1 kg (2 lb 4 oz)
1 onion, quartered
1 carrot, cut into 8 pieces
1 celery stalk
2 bay leaves
1 tablespoon red wine vinegar
1 slice of bread, crusts removed
4 tablespoons milk
1 hard-boiled egg
60 g (2 oz/3 cups) fresh flat-leaf parsley
Juice of 1 lemon
6 anchovies
3 garlic cloves, peeled and left whole
250 ml (9 fl oz/1 cup) extra virgin olive oil,
  plus 2 tablespoons extra for frying
Sea salt and freshly ground black pepper
2 tablespoons Sicilian capers, soaked and
  desalted (see page 36), chopped

PARSNIP PUREE

500 g (1 lb 2 oz) parsnips, cored, cubed
6 garlic cloves, peeled and left whole
50 g (2 oz) unsalted butter
8 tablespoons extra virgin olive oil
2 tablespoons grated parmesan cheese
Sea salt and white pepper

METHOD

FOR THE GRILLED OX TONGUE WITH SALSA VERDE / Place the tongue in a large pot with the onion, carrot, celery, bay leaves and vinegar. Cover with water and bring to the boil. Turn down the heat, cover and keep simmering for 90–120 minutes until the tongue is cooked, which is when the skin peels off easily. Once cooked, let the tongue cool in the cooking liquid, then refrigerate. To make the salsa verde, moisten the bread with the milk until it is completely absorbed. Place the bread, hard-boiled egg, parsley, lemon juice, anchovies and garlic cloves into a food processor and turn it on. Slowly pour in the extra virgin olive oil until it is well blended. Season with salt, mix in the capers and store in a jar in the refrigerator until needed. Remove the salsa verde from the refrigerator at least an hour before use. Peel the skin totally from the cooked tongue and trim any fat at the base. Slice thinly into 24 slices across. Any left-over slices can be stored in their cooking liquid in the refrigerator for 6 days.

FOR THE PARSNIP PUREE / Place all the parsnips and peeled garlic cloves in a large pot and just cover with cold water. Bring to the boil, then simmer for 25 minutes. Drain, setting the water aside for later. In a food processor, pulse the parsnips and garlic with the butter, extra virgin olive oil and parmesan until they are well blended. Add a little of the cooking water to give a rich, thick and creamy consistency. Season with salt and fine white pepper to taste and stir until well incorporated. Any leftover can be stored in the refrigerator for 5 days.

TO ASSEMBLE / Place the Roman pizza squares on a baking tray and heat in a preheated 180°C (350°F) oven for 5–6 minutes until they are crisp on the outside but soft in the middle. Meanwhile, chargrill the ox tongue by heating the remaining olive oil in a chargrill pan and searing the slices for 30 seconds each side. Once the squares are ready, remove from the oven. Place the squares on the work surface and spread 2 tablespoons parsnip purée on each, then put 3 slices of grilled ox tongue on top and spoon ½ tablespoon salsa verde on top of that.

Makes 8 squares

THIS PAGE / Looking south along the Naples coastline.

Roman pizza with vitello tonnato

I love vitello tonnato (veal in tuna sauce) with crusty bread, so this Roman pizza is a favourite. My method of preparing it uses an improvised sous vide, or low-temperature water bath, to cook the veal. If you actually have a sous vide, better still. It results in moist, pink meat with lots of flavour.

INGREDIENTS

1 sheet of Roman-style pizza dough
 (see pages 84–88), precooked
 (see page 89) and cut into 8 squares

8 Treviso radicchio leaves, cut into strips

VITELLO TONNATO
600–800 g (1 lb 5 oz–1 lb 12 oz) veal
 'girello' (eye of round), cut into 2 pieces
4 tablespoons extra virgin olive oil
100 ml (3½ fl oz) dry white wine
2 small garlic cloves, crushed
2 bay leaves
2 small fresh parsley stems
2 whole cloves
2 teaspoons grated lemon rind
Sea salt and freshly ground black pepper
150 g (5½ oz) tinned tuna, drained and
 roughly chopped
4 anchovies, drained and roughly chopped
250 g (9 oz/1 cup) mayonnaise
25 g (1 oz) Sicilian capers, soaked and
 desalted (see page 36)
4 tablespoons fresh parsley, finely chopped

FRIED CAPERS
2 tablespoons Sicilian capers, soaked and
 desalted (see page 36)
50–100 ml (2–3½ fl oz/⅓ cup) extra virgin
 olive oil

METHOD

FOR THE VITELLO TONNATO / Preheat the oven to 60°C (140°F) and place a deep, wide bowl filled two-thirds with water in for at least 30 minutes so the water reaches the same temperature as the oven. Place the two pieces of veal in two separate snap-lock plastic bags with equal amounts of the extra virgin olive oil, white wine, garlic, bay leaves, parsley stems, cloves and lemon rind. Season with salt and pepper and seal, making sure that most of the air is squeezed out of the bag before closing. Place each bag in another snap-lock bag for security, pressing the air out of the second bag as well before sealing. Put the bags carefully in the preheated water bath, making sure they are submerged. A plate may be needed to keep the bags under the water. Cook for 5 hours. Afterwards, carefully remove the bowl containing the water. Remove the bags from the water bath and place in a large bowl or bucket in which there is plenty of ice and cold water. Cool the bags for 10–15 minutes before removing the meat from the bags, straining the cooking juices through muslin (cheesecloth) and cutting into 32 thin slices. To make the sauce, mix the tuna and anchovies with 125 ml (4 fl oz) of the cooled strained cooking juices and whisk into the mayonnaise. Add the capers and parsley and season with salt, if necessary.

FOR THE FRIED CAPERS / Dry the capers by patting with a paper towel. Place 1 cm (½ inch) olive oil in the smallest saucepan you can find so you'll use as little oil as possible. Heat until the oil begins to move on its surface. Test by adding a caper. If it sizzles and fries, the oil's hot enough. Add all the capers, fry for 30 seconds, then remove with a slotted spoon to a plate lined with paper towels. These will last for a few days on paper towel in a covered container.

TO ASSEMBLE / Cut each pizza square in half, opening it to form a 'sandwich'. Place the halves back together on a baking tray and heat in a preheated 180°C (350°F) oven for about 5–6 minutes until they are crisp on the outside but soft in the middle. Once ready, remove from the oven. Place the bottom of each square on the work surface and lay the radicchio strips on top. Now place 4 slices of vitello on each and dress with the tuna mayonnaise and some cooled fried capers. Close the 'sandwich' with the top half to finish.

Makes 8 filled Roman pizze

Roman pizza with eggplant parmigiana

Everybody loves a good eggplant parmigiana. This is a homage to that great dish, albeit in the shape of a Roman pizza.

INGREDIENTS

1 sheet of Roman-style pizza dough
(see pages 84–88), precooked
(see page 89) and cut into 8 squares

8 slices of fior di latte mozzarella
16 slices of smoked scamorza cheese
24 slices of chargrilled eggplant
(aubergine) (see page 98)
8 tablespoons grated parmesan cheese
2 tablespoons shaved parmesan cheese
24 confit tomatoes (see page 152)
8 sprigs of fresh basil

SAN MARZANO SAUCE
4 tablespoons extra virgin olive oil
1 onion, minced
2 garlic cloves, crushed
650 g (1 lb 7 oz/2½ cups) tinned San
Marzano whole peeled tomatoes,
puréed
25 g (1 oz/½ cup) fresh basil leaves,
roughly torn
Sea salt and freshly ground black pepper

METHOD

FOR THE SAN MARZANO SAUCE / Heat the olive oil in a pan and gently fry the onion and garlic until transparent. Add the tomato and basil. Season with a couple of pinches of salt and a little pepper. Stir well and simmer slowly until the sauce thickens and most of the water has evaporated. Depending on the tomatoes, this should take 10–15 minutes. Any extra tomato sauce can be stored in the refrigerator for 5–6 days.

TO ASSEMBLE / Cut each pizza square in half, opening it to form a 'sandwich'. Place the halves on a baking tray. On the bottom half of each place one slice of mozzarella and two slices of scamorza. Heat in a preheated 180°C (350°F) oven for 4–5 minutes until they are crisp on the outside but soft in the middle and the cheese has melted. Once ready, remove from the oven and on each bottom half place three pieces of chargrilled eggplant, 2 tablespoons San Marzano sauce and a tablespoon of grated parmesan. Close each with the top half of the pizza square and finish with some shaved parmesan, three confit tomatoes and a sprig of basil.

Makes 8 filled Roman pizze

Roman pizza filled with cavolo nero frittata and 'nduja

When my brother and I would come home from school or after playing all day, my mother would make a frittata in what seemed like an instant. It was her quick fix for two hungry boys. As I grew up, my friends at school would have their egg sandwiches and I had my frittata sandwich. This recalls that very sandwich, with the grown-up addition of spicy 'nduja. Cavolo nero is also called Tuscan black kale. Tender spinach leaves can be substituted.

INGREDIENTS

1 sheet of Roman-style pizza dough
   (see pages 84–88), precooked
   (see page 89) and cut into 8 squares

4 tablespoons 'nduja
70 g (2½ oz/2 cups) young rocket
   (arugula) leaves, trimmed
2 tablespoons extra virgin olive oil

CAVOLO NERO FRITTATA
4 large leaves of cavolo nero,
   stems removed
12 large eggs
Sea salt and freshly ground black pepper
4 tablespoons grated parmesan cheese
2 tablespoons chopped fresh parsley
4 tablespoons extra virgin olive oil
2 small leeks, washed thoroughly and cut
   into thin rounds
2 garlic cloves, crushed

METHOD

FOR THE CAVOLO NERO FRITTATA / Bring a pot of water to the boil and plunge in the trimmed cavolo nero leaves. Boil for 3 minutes, then drain and let cool. Chop the leaves. Crack the eggs into a bowl. Add salt and pepper, beat lightly, then add the parmesan, chopped parsley and the cavolo nero. Beat lightly to mix the ingredients. Heat half the olive oil in a pan and lightly fry half the leek and garlic until soft. This should take about 2 minutes. Add half the egg mixture to the pan. Lift the edges as it cooks and firms up with a spatula. Keep doing this for about 90 seconds on a medium–high heat. Turn the frittata and cook the other side for a minute or so until the middle feels firm to the touch. Allow the frittata to cool in the pan before repeating with the remaining ingredients to make a second.

TO ASSEMBLE / Cut each pizza square in half, opening it to form a 'sandwich'. Place the halves back together on a baking tray and heat in a preheated 180°C (350°F) oven for about 5–6 minutes until they are crisp on the outside but soft in the middle. Once ready, remove from the oven. Spread a little 'nduja on the underside of the top half of each square. Place the bottom halves on serving plates or wooden boards and first place some rocket leaves on top, then a quarter of a frittata. Sprinkle with extra virgin olive oil and close with the top half of the square.

Makes 8 filled Roman pizze

Roman pizza with pork belly, pickled onion and fig jam

One of the joys of eating on the street in Italy is the large number of versions of the panino (bread roll) filled with slices of herby porchetta encased in blistered, crunchy crackling. A whole roast pig or pork loin porchetta can take a couple of days to prepare, but the belly is achievable in a shorter time.

INGREDIENTS

1 sheet of Roman-style pizza dough
 (see pages 84–88), precooked
 (see page 89) and cut into 8 squares

16 slices of fior di latte mozzarella
70 g (2½ oz/2 cups) rocket (arugula),
 thick stems removed
8 tablespoons pickled red onion
 (see page 150)
2 tablespoons extra virgin olive oil

SLOW-ROASTED PORK BELLY
2 tablespoons fresh rosemary leaves
2 tablespoons fresh sage leaves
6 fennel seeds
2 garlic cloves
1 whole pork belly, about 800 g
 (1 lb 12 oz), skin on
2 tablespoons sea salt
1 teaspoon freshly ground black pepper
500 ml (17 fl oz/2 cups) white wine

FIG JAM
100 g (3½ oz/⅓ cup) honey
1 cinnamon stick
4 cloves
1 vanilla bean, split lengthways and seeds
 scraped
500 g (1 lb 2 oz) fresh figs

METHOD

FOR THE SLOW-ROASTED PORK BELLY / Chop the herbs with the garlic using a knife, not a food processor. Place the belly, skin side down, on a work surface and make small incisions all around the thickest part of the meat. In each little hole, sprinkle salt, pepper and some herbs, so the herbs penetrate into the meat. Cover the skin side of the belly with remaining salt, pepper and herbs. Place the belly, skin side up, on a rack over a tray in the fridge and allow the moisture from the meat to drain out overnight. The next day, take the belly out of the fridge for an hour to come to room temperature before cooking for at least 3 hours in a roasting pan in a preheated 130°C (250°F) oven. Check regularly and pour in about 50 ml (2 fl oz) of wine every 45 minutes – this will keep the meat moist. When the belly is cooked, drain off the cooking juices and reserve. Turn up the heat to 200°C (400°F) and cook the belly in the oven for 20–30 minutes until the skin crackles. Remove the belly and cut into thin slices. Any extra slow-roasted pork can be stored in the refrigerator for 4–5 days.

FOR THE FIG JAM / Heat the honey, cinnamon, cloves and vanilla in a large pan. Chop each fig into six. When the honey comes to the boil, stir in the figs and turn down to a simmer. Simmer gently for about 30 minutes until thick and jam-like. Remove from the heat. Cool a little before transferring to a sterilised jar. This makes about 500 g (1 lb 2 oz) jam, which will store in the refrigerator for up to 4 months.

TO ASSEMBLE / Cut each pizza square in half, opening it to form a 'sandwich'. Place the halves on a baking tray. On the bottom half of each place two slices of mozzarella and heat in a preheated 180°C (350°F) oven for about 4–5 minutes until they are crisp on the outside but soft in the middle and the cheese has melted. Once ready, remove from the oven. Place the bottom halves on serving plates or boards and fill each with the rocket, then a slice of pork, cut in half, 1 tablespoon of the jam and onion. Sprinkle with olive oil and close with the top half of the square. Finish with a dollop of fig jam and some onion on top.

Makes 8 filled Roman pizze

Roman pizza with silverbeet, field mushrooms and fontina

Silverbeet, or Swiss chard, prepared in this combination with mushrooms and fontina is a dish that I enjoy on steaming polenta. And when the silverbeet is young and tender, the stalks are excellent for the texture as well as the bittersweet flavour they impart. Choose large, meaty mushrooms for this. They should feel heavy in your hand. If you can get fresh porcini mushrooms, all the better.

INGREDIENTS

1 sheet of Roman-style pizza dough (see pages 84–88), precooked (see page 89) and left whole or cut into 8 squares

300 g (10½ oz) fontina cheese, thinly sliced
2 tablespoons grated parmesan cheese
2 tablespoons chopped fresh parsley
2 tablespoons extra virgin olive oil

BRAISED SILVERBEET
12 young silverbeet (Swiss chard) leaves, stems intact
2 tablespoons extra virgin olive oil
1 garlic clove, crushed, keeping it in one piece
80 ml (2½ fl oz/⅓ cup) dry white wine
Sea salt and freshly ground black pepper

PAN-FRIED FIELD MUSHROOMS
3–4 tablespoons extra virgin olive oil
Extra virgin olive oil, for frying
6–8 large field mushrooms, cut into 1 cm (½ inch) thick slices
Sea salt

METHOD

FOR THE BRAISED SILVERBEET / Fill a large pot three-quarters full of water. Add a teaspoon of salt and bring to the boil, covered. Meanwhile, trim the very bottom of the silverbeet stems and discard. Wash the silverbeet well. Once the water is boiling, plunge in the silverbeet, using a wooden spoon to keep the silverbeet submerged. Once the water comes back to the boil, turn down to a simmer and cook for 2 minutes. Drain. In a wide braising pan, heat the olive oil and add the garlic. When the garlic begins to fry, add the well-drained silverbeet leaves intact and move them around carefully in the pan without breaking them for 1 minute. Add the wine and continue to cook until the liquid has completely disappeared. Season with salt and pepper and take off the heat. Place aside to cool. Any left-over silverbeet can be refrigerated for 2–3 days.

FOR THE PAN-FRIED FIELD MUSHROOMS / Heat 2 tablespoons olive oil in a wide pan. Once the oil begins to smoke, place the mushroom slices in carefully, in batches if necessary. After 20–30 seconds, turn them to cook on the other side for 10–15 seconds. Place on a plate covered with paper towel and season lightly with salt. Heat more oil, as needed, and repeat with the remaining mushrooms. Any left-over mushrooms can be refrigerated for 2–3 days.

TO ASSEMBLE / Place the Roman pizza sheet or squares on a baking tray. Distribute the fontina slices on top and sprinkle with the parmesan. Evenly spread the braised silverbeet on top, then the pan-fried mushrooms and bake in a preheated 180°C (350°F) oven for 10 minutes. Once cooked, remove from the oven and place on a wooden board or serving plate as a large piece or cut into tiles, using scissors, and plate individually. Sprinkle with the parsley and finish with extra virgin olive oil.

Makes 8 squares

Roman pizza with tuna tartare

Raw seafood, called 'crudo' rather than 'carpaccio', is used by many of the protagonists in the 'new pizza' movement in Italy, both on the round wood-fired and the Roman teglia types. The seafood needs to be super fresh and the pizza consumed immediately.

INGREDIENTS

1 sheet of Roman-style pizza dough
    (see pages 84–88), precooked
    (see page 89) and cut into 8 squares

2 teaspoons thinly sliced fresh chives

TUNA TARTARE
80 g (3 oz/½ cup) seedless raisins
800 g (1 lb 12 oz) tuna fillet, bloodline
    removed
8 anchovies, drained and finely chopped
80 g (3 oz/½ cup) pine nuts, toasted and
    roughly chopped
1 tablespoon Sicilian capers, soaked and
    desalted (see page 36), chopped
6 tablespoons extra virgin olive oil
Sea salt and freshly ground black pepper

METHOD

FOR THE TUNA TARTARE / Place the raisins in a bowl and cover with tepid water for 30 minutes. Drain and pat them dry. Meanwhile, cut the tuna carefully into 5 mm (¼ inch) cubes and place in a bowl. Chop the raisins and add to the tuna along with the anchovies, pine nuts, capers and olive oil. Mix well and season to taste with salt and pepper. Cover with plastic wrap and refrigerate for at least an hour.

TO ASSEMBLE / Place the Roman pizza squares on a baking tray and heat in a preheated 180°C (350°F) oven for about 5–6 minutes until they are crisp on the outside but soft in the middle. Meanwhile, remove the tuna tartare from the refrigerator. When the pizza squares are ready, remove from the oven, place on serving plates and evenly distribute the tuna tartare on top. Sprinkle with the sliced chives and finish by dressing with a little of the liquid left over from the tuna tartare.

Makes 8 squares

THIS PAGE / Fishing boats moored off Cetara.

LAN'ZA

(PREDRESSED)

As well as precooking the pizza sheet, or 'teglia', and then filling or topping it, the Roman-style pizza dough can be dressed before cooking to give a different effect, closer to the Neapolitan pizza. It may then be finished with more ingredients once cooked. For this 'predressed' pizza, use the same dough as for the 'precooked' Roman pizze in the previous chapter.

Roman pizza margherita

Although on a Roman-style base, this tomato-topped pizza has the same ingredients as a classic Naples Margherita. The main difference is that the mozzarella is torn in pieces and scattered on the surface after it's taken from the oven.

INGREDIENTS

1 sheet of Roman-style pizza dough
(see pages 84–88)

350 g (12 oz/1⅓ cups) tinned San
Marzano whole peeled tomatoes
2 tablespoons extra virgin olive oil
Pinch of sea salt
400 g (14 oz) fior di latte mozzarella
100 g (3½ oz/2 cups) fresh basil leaves

METHOD

TO ASSEMBLE / Preheat the oven to 220°C (425°F). Hand squeeze the tomatoes until they're uniformly mashed and mix in a tablespoon of extra virgin olive oil and a pinch of salt. Spread the tomato mixture on top of the sheet of pizza as evenly as possible. If the dough has risen excessively, press down gently with the tips of your fingers to make small indentations to trap the tomato. Bake in the oven for 25 minutes. If the teglia is browning more on one side, your oven is not even and the tray may need to be turned. Once cooked, remove from the oven and let cool a little. Place on a serving plate as a large piece or cut, using scissors, into individual tiles. Remove the mozzarella from the water. Tear into small pieces and distribute on top of the pizza. Scatter the basil leaves on top and finish with the remaining extra virgin olive oil.

Serves 6–8

Roman pizza with zucchini trifolati

Many of the toppings on these pizze are built on memories from my childhood. In discussing this particular pizza with Pizzaperta chef Gianluca, we discovered we had similar memories of zucchini (courgette) trifolati. Both our mothers prepared this dish in a similar way, though at different ends of the peninsula – Brescia and Naples. 'Trifolati' is an Italian cooking term that denotes frying in olive oil, garlic and parsley. It is most often applied to mushrooms, kidneys and zucchini.

INGREDIENTS

1 sheet of Roman-style pizza dough
(see pages 84–88)

350 g (12 oz) fior di latte mozzarella
Sea salt and freshly ground black pepper
1 tablespoon extra virgin olive oil

ZUCCHINI TRIFOLATI
1 small onion, thinly sliced
500 g (1 lb 2 oz) zucchini (courgettes),
cut into thin rounds
2 garlic cloves, crushed
3 tablespoons extra virgin olive oil
2 tinned San Marzano whole peeled
tomatoes, chopped
2 tablespoons finely chopped fresh
flat-leaf parsley
Sea salt and freshly ground black pepper

METHOD

FOR THE ZUCCHINI TRIFOLATI / Fry the onion, zucchini and garlic in the olive oil for 2 minutes over a high heat, keeping them stirred so they don't colour. Add the tomato and simmer for 15 minutes. Add the chopped parsley, season with salt and pepper and mix well. Leave to cool completely. Any left-over zucchini can be refrigerated for 3–4 days.

TO ASSEMBLE / Preheat the oven to 220°C (425°F). Place the cooked and cooled zucchini trifolati in a sieve to drain its liquid, saving some of the liquid. Remove the mozzarella from the water. Tear into small pieces and distribute half on top of the sheet of pizza. Scatter 400 g (14 oz) of the well-drained zucchini trifolati on the mozzarella. Distribute the rest of the torn mozzarella on the zucchini. Finally, season with a little salt and freshly ground black pepper and drizzle with the olive oil. If the dough has risen excessively, press down gently with the tips of your fingers to make small indentations to make space for the mozzarella and zucchini. Bake in the oven for 25 minutes. If the teglia is browning more on one side, your oven is not even and the tray may need to be turned. Once cooked, remove from oven and let cool a little. Place on a serving plate as a large piece or cut, using scissors, into individual tiles. Finish by drizzling with some of the zucchini trifolati juices that have been drained.

Serves 6–8

Roman pizza with baba ganoush and prawns

Baba ganoush is the famous Middle Eastern preparation made from eggplant (aubergine), sesame paste (tahini), garlic and olive oil. I make it regularly to spread on crusty bread with countless other things on top. In this case it's being served with prawns (shrimp), but it would go just as well with scallops, octopus or lamb shoulder.

INGREDIENTS

1 sheet of Roman-style pizza dough
 (see pages 84–88)

350 g (12 oz/1⅓ cups) tinned San
 Marzano whole peeled tomatoes
2 tablespoons extra virgin olive oil
Sea salt
32 medium prawns (shrimp), shelled
2 tablespoons finely chopped fresh parsley

BABA GANOUSH

3 large eggplants (aubergines)
2 tablespoons tahini
2 tablespoons lemon juice
2 garlic cloves
Sea salt
2 tablespoons extra virgin olive oil
1 teaspoon smoked paprika
1 tablespoon finely chopped fresh
 flat-leaf parsley

METHOD

FOR THE BABA GANOUSH / Place each eggplant over a gas flame, turning until the skin is evenly charred and the flesh is soft all the way to the centre. Remove and place on a plate to cool for 10–15 minutes. Cut the eggplants in half, top to bottom, scoop out the flesh and place in a colander to drain for 15–20 minutes. Place the eggplant in a food processor with the tahini, lemon juice, garlic and salt and process until smooth. Add extra tahini, lemon juice or salt to taste. Spoon into a bowl and add the olive oil so it covers the top. Sprinkle the smoked paprika and parsley over. Any left-over baba ganoush can be refrigerated for 3–4 days.

TO ASSEMBLE / Preheat the oven to 220°C (425°F). Hand squeeze the tomatoes until they're uniformly mashed and mix in a tablespoon of olive oil and a pinch of salt. Spread the tomato mixture on top of the sheet of pizza as evenly as possible. If the dough has risen excessively, press down gently with the tips of your fingers to make small indentations to trap the tomato. Bake in the oven for 25 minutes. If the teglia is browning more on one side, your oven is not even and the tray may need to be turned. While the teglia is cooking, heat the remaining olive oil in a pan. When it begins to smoke, add half the prawns and fry until just cooked. Remove the cooked prawns and place on a plate, seasoning with salt. Fry the remaining prawns the same way. Reserve any cooking juices. Once the teglia is cooked, remove from the oven and let cool a little. Place on a serving plate as a large piece or cut, using scissors, into individual tiles. Spoon baba ganoush over the surface, then place the prawns on top. Scatter with the parsley and finish by sprinkling the prawn cooking juices over the lot.

Serves 6–8

Roman pizza with roast beef, shiitake and grana

This is a meal in itself. Remember to rest your beef well, allowing the juices to 'set' internally so that when it's cut it won't 'bleed'. This recipe will result in rare roast beef. If you prefer it cooked more, simply leave it in the oven for an extra 2 minutes for medium rare. I like the flavour of shiitake mushrooms with roast beef but if you prefer, use other mushrooms instead.

INGREDIENTS

1 sheet of Roman-style pizza dough
   (see pages 84–88)

350 g (12 oz/1⅓ cups) tinned San
   Marzano whole peeled tomatoes
1 tablespoon extra virgin olive oil
Pinch of sea salt
Salsa verde (see page 166)
95 g (3½ oz/1 cup) Grana Padano
   cheese shavings

ROAST BEEF
1 kg (2 lb 4 oz) piece of beef fillet, trimmed
Sea salt and freshly ground black pepper
1 tablespoon extra virgin olive oil

BRAISED SHIITAKE MUSHROOMS
2 tablespoons extra virgin olive oil
2 garlic cloves, crushed
500 g (1 lb 2 oz) fresh shiitake mushrooms,
   stems trimmed
Sea salt
125 ml (4 fl oz/½ cup) dry white wine

METHOD

FOR THE ROAST BEEF / Preheat the oven to 220°C (425°F). Remove the beef from the refrigerator 20 minutes before cooking. Season the beef with a pinch of salt and a little ground pepper. Heat the olive oil in a heavy-based frying pan and sear the meat until it is well browned on all sides. Place the pan, with meat, in the oven for 4–5 minutes, turning the fillet in the pan after 2 minutes. Remove and rest in the pan to cool. Once cool and ready to dress the pizza, slice the beef into 16 pieces. It should be rare.

FOR THE BRAISED SHIITAKE MUSHROOMS / Heat the olive oil in a braising pan and add the garlic. Stir for 15–20 seconds. Turn up the heat and add the mushrooms and a couple of good pinches of salt. Continue to stir for 3–4 minutes until the mushrooms have softened. Add the wine. Once the wine begins to boil, turn down to a simmer and continue cooking for about 5 minutes until the mushrooms are tender. Remove from the heat and season with salt to taste. Mix thoroughly and let cool. Once cool, drain the mushrooms from their liquid. Any left-over mushrooms can be refrigerated for 3–4 days.

TO ASSEMBLE / Preheat the oven to 220°C (425°F). Hand squeeze the tomatoes until they're uniformly mashed and mix in the extra virgin olive oil and a pinch of salt. Spread the tomato mixture on top of the dough as evenly as possible. If the dough has risen excessively, press down gently with the tips of your fingers to make small indentations to trap the tomato. Bake in the oven for 25 minutes. If the teglia is browning more on one side, your oven is not even and the tray may need to be turned. Once cooked, remove from the oven and let cool a little. Place on a serving plate as a large piece or cut, using scissors, into individual tiles. Begin by putting two slices of roast beef on each tile, then scatter the braised shiitake liberally on top and dress with the salsa verde. Finish with the Grana Padano shavings.

Serves 6–8

Roman pizza with gorgonzola and figs

If you've ever had a dry red wine with gorgonzola, or other sharp blue cheeses, you'll know that it's not a great match. A reaction occurs whereby a metallic-like taste is left in your mouth. Sweet things are far more complementary, like sweet wine and, in this case, figs. Choose figs that are at the peak of their ripeness and sweetness.

INGREDIENTS

1 sheet of Roman-style pizza dough
(see pages 84–88)

20 ripe green or black figs
2 tablespoons extra virgin olive oil
200 g (7 oz) gorgonzola piccante cheese

METHOD

TO ASSEMBLE / Preheat the oven to 220°C (425°F). Peel half the figs and cut each into six top to bottom. Cut the rest the same way, but leave them unpeeled. Take the sheet of pizza, scatter the peeled figs evenly over the sheet and sprinkle over the extra virgin olive oil. If the dough has risen excessively, press down gently with the tips of your fingers to make the surface flat to hold the figs. Bake in the oven for 25 minutes. If the teglia is browning more on one side, your oven is not even and the tray may need to be turned. The figs should be soft and partly caramelised. Once cooked, remove from the oven and let cool a little. Place on a serving plate as a large piece or cut, using scissors, into individual tiles. Distribute the remaining unpeeled fig segments on top. Cut the gorgonzola into small pieces and distribute on top of the pizza.

Serves 6–8

Roman pizza with cavolo nero, mushrooms and lardo

Lardo is the Italian word for pork back fat that has been salted, cured with herbs and spices and then dried. It must be mother-of-pearl white and smell and taste sweet. It should be sliced very thin and, when eaten, it should melt in the mouth. Make the cavolo nero and mushroom mix as close to serving time as possible. Failing that, make it in advance and reheat. The mixture must be hot, or at least warm, to melt the lardo slightly.

INGREDIENTS

1 sheet of Roman-style pizza dough
   (see pages 84–88)

350 g (12 oz/1⅓ cups) tinned San
   Marzano whole peeled tomatoes
1 tablespoon extra virgin olive oil
Pinch of salt
95 g (3½ oz/1 cup) parmesan
   cheese shavings
32 thin slices of lardo

CAVOLO NERO AND MUSHROOMS

20 g (¾ oz) dried porcini mushrooms
500 g (1 lb 2 oz) cavolo nero,
   stems removed
3 tablespoons extra virgin olive oil
2 garlic cloves, crushed
1 small white onion, finely chopped
300 g (10½ oz) button or Swiss brown
   mushrooms, sliced
150 g (5½ oz) shiitake mushrooms, sliced
3 tablespoons finely chopped fresh parsley
Sea salt and freshly ground black pepper

METHOD

FOR THE CAVOLO NERO AND MUSHROOMS / First soak the dried porcini in a small bowl of cold water for 10–15 minutes until soft. Drain and chop them. Bring a pot of water to a rolling boil and blanch the cavolo nero leaves for 90 seconds. Drain well. Heat 2 tablespoons of the oil in a pan and gently fry the garlic and onion together for a minute. Add the mushrooms and fry over a medium heat, constantly stirring, until they have softened. Add the parsley and cavolo nero, season to taste with salt and pepper and stir well. After simmering for a moment more, turn off the heat. Any left-over mixture can be refrigerated for 3–4 days.

TO ASSEMBLE / Preheat the oven to 220°C (425°F). Hand squeeze the tomatoes until they're uniformly mashed and mix in the extra virgin olive oil and a pinch of salt. Spread the tomato mixture on top of the sheet of pizza as evenly as possible. If the dough has risen excessively, press down gently with the tips of your fingers to make small indentations to trap the tomato. Bake in the oven for 25 minutes. If the teglia is browning more on one side, your oven is not even and the tray may need to be turned. Once cooked, remove from the oven and let cool a little. Place on a serving plate as a large piece or cut, using scissors, into individual tiles. Spread the warm–hot cavolo nero and mushroom mixture evenly over the pizza. Scatter the shavings of parmesan across the top and finally drape the lardo slices over. The heat of the mixture will melt the lardo a little, so it becomes transparent. Serve immediately.

Serves 6–8

Roman pizza with cuttlefish, broccoli and chilli

Cuttlefish is often seen as a poor version of calamari (squid). In truth they are very different and both equally delicious. Cuttlefish is thicker, meatier and more pronounced in flavour. It matches and complements the bold flavours in this dish, especially with the addition of the colatura d'alici (anchovy sauce).

INGREDIENTS

1 sheet of Roman-style pizza dough
(see pages 84–88)

350 g (12 oz/1⅓ cups) tinned San
Marzano whole peeled tomatoes
2 tablespoons extra virgin olive oil
500 g (1 lb 2 oz) cleaned cuttlefish,
cut into 1 cm (½ inch) wide strips
2 red chillies, sliced
1 teaspoon colatura d'alici

PAN-FRIED BROCCOLI

600 g (1 lb 5 oz) broccoli, trimmed of
woody stalks
3 tablespoons extra virgin olive oil
1 onion, finely diced
2 garlic cloves, crushed
Sea salt and freshly ground black pepper

METHOD

FOR THE PAN-FRIED BROCCOLI / Cut the broccoli heads into florets and stalks into 1 cm (½ inch) lengths. Bring a pot of water to a rolling boil and blanch the broccoli for 90 seconds. Drain well. Heat the olive oil in a large pan and gently fry the onion and garlic until soft. Turn the heat up to moderate and add the broccoli, stirring constantly for about 4 minutes until tender. Season with a couple of good pinches of salt and a little ground pepper.

TO ASSEMBLE / Preheat the oven to 220°C (425°F). Hand squeeze the tomatoes until they're uniformly mashed and mix in a tablespoon of extra virgin olive oil and a pinch of salt. Spread the tomato mixture on top of the dough as evenly as possible. If the dough has risen excessively, press down gently with the tips of your fingers to make small indentations to trap the tomato. Bake in the oven for 25 minutes. If the teglia is browning more on one side, your oven is not even and the tray may need to be turned. While the pizza is cooking, heat the remaining olive oil in a wide heavy-based frying pan. Once the oil begins to smoke, carefully add the cuttlefish and chilli and cook quickly for a minute or so, continually moving them in the pan. Once the teglia sheet is cooked, remove from the oven and let cool a little. Place on a serving plate as a large piece or cut, using scissors, into individual tiles. Scatter with the pan-fried broccoli and the fried cuttlefish. Mix the colatura d'alici with 125 ml (4 fl oz) of the cuttlefish cooking juices and spoon over the top as a final dressing.

Serves 6–8

OPPOSITE / Wild fennel flowers and pollen on the Alta Murgia in Puglia. **THIS PAGE** / Afternoons in Altamura, Puglia.

Roman pizza with red onion

This is more of a snack pizza, which can be cut into fingers and eaten with antipasto or served as a base for topping with things like caponata, chopped roast vegetables, salami or even cooked sausage.

INGREDIENTS

1 sheet of Roman-style pizza dough
  (see pages 84–88)

2 tablespoons extra virgin olive oil
1 kg (2 lb 4 oz) red onions, thinly sliced
Sea salt and freshly ground black pepper

METHOD

TO ASSEMBLE / Heat the olive oil in a heavy-based frying pan and gently fry the onion for 2 minutes. Remove from the heat, season to taste and let the onion cool. Preheat the oven to 220°C (425°F). Spread the onion on top of the sheet of pizza as evenly as possible. If the dough has risen excessively, press down gently with the tips of your fingers to make small indentations. If there is any oil in the pan from cooking the onion, scatter it on top of the dough. Bake in the oven for 25 minutes. If the teglia is browning more on one side, your oven is not even and the tray may need to be turned. Once cooked, remove from the oven and the pizza is ready to use. It can be cut into pieces and used as bread or topped with anything appropriate. It can also be wrapped and stored in the refrigerator for up to 4 days and is excellent reheated.

Serves 6–8

Roman pizza with potato and braised beef cheeks

Here's a pizza for the cold days of winter when we long for slow-cooked, gelatinous dishes such as osso buco and oxtail. These beef cheeks have a good deal of pepper in their preparation and, combined with the potato on top of a crisp and airy pizza tile, they become a complete dish.

INGREDIENTS

1 sheet of Roman-style pizza dough
(see pages 84–88)

500 g (1 lb 2 oz) yellow-fleshed waxy
potatoes, such as Spunta, Nicola
or Desiree
2 tablespoons extra virgin olive oil
Sea salt
2 tablespoons finely chopped fresh parsley

BRAISED PEPPERED BEEF CHEEKS
2 kg (4 lb 8 oz) beef cheeks, cut into 2 cm
(¾ inch) cubes
4 garlic cloves, lightly crushed
1 red onion, cut into 1 cm (½ inch) cubes
1 carrot, cut into 1 cm (½ inch) cubes
2 celery stalks, cut into 1 cm (½ inch) cubes
1 litre (35 fl oz/4 cups) dry red wine
1 tablespoon freshly ground black pepper
1 tablespoon tomato paste (concentrated
puree)
2 bay leaves
500 ml (17 fl oz/2 cups) veal stock
Sea salt

METHOD

FOR THE BRAISED PEPPERED BEEF CHEEKS / Place the cubed beef in a casserole dish with the garlic, onion, carrot, celery and enough wine to just cover the meat. Bring to a simmer and keep simmering for 2 hours, partly covered with a lid. Add the pepper, tomato paste, bay leaves, the rest of the wine and the veal stock. Add two to three good pinches of salt and stir in. Keep simmering gently, uncovered, for 2 or more hours until the sauce has reduced and thickened. If it dries out too much and catches on the bottom, stir in a little more stock. When cooked, check the seasoning and add a little more salt, if needed. Any left-over beef cheeks can be frozen or refrigerated for up to 6 days.

TO ASSEMBLE / Scrub the potatoes so the skins are clean. Place in a pot and cover with water. Cover the pot with a lid and bring to the boil. Turn down to a simmer and keep cooking until the potatoes are soft: a skewer should easily pierce them all the way to the centre. Remove from the heat and drain, letting the potatoes cool. Peel the potatoes and break the flesh apart with your fingers. Place in a bowl and mix with the extra virgin olive oil and some salt. Preheat the oven to 220°C (425°F). Spread the potatoes on top of the sheet of pizza as evenly as possible. If the dough has risen excessively, press down gently with the tips of your fingers to make small indentations. Bake in the oven for 25 minutes. If the teglia is browning more on one side, your oven is not even and the tray may need to be turned. Once cooked, remove from the oven and let cool a little. Cut into eight individual tiles and place on serving plates. Distribute about half the warm braised beef cheeks here and there, over the potatoes, spooning a little of the sauce on top. Sprinkle with the parsley.

Makes 8 squares

Roman pizza with tomato and stracciatella

This is such a simple pizza, dressed with few ingredients. The stracciatella makes the preparation luxuriously rich and creamy.

INGREDIENTS

1 sheet of Roman-style pizza dough
   (see pages 84–88)

300 g (10½ oz/1¼ cups) tinned San
   Marzano peeled tomatoes
2 tablespoons extra virgin olive oil
Sea salt and freshly ground black pepper
350 g (12 oz) stracciatella cheese
50 g (2 oz/1 cup) fresh basil leaves

METHOD

TO ASSEMBLE / Preheat the oven to 220°C (425°F). Hand squeeze the tomatoes until they're uniformly mashed and mix in a tablespoon of extra virgin olive oil and a pinch of salt. Spread the tomato mixture on top of the sheet of pizza as evenly as possible. If the dough has risen excessively, press down gently with the tips of your fingers to make small indentations to trap the tomato. Bake in the oven for 25 minutes. If the teglia is browning more on one side, your oven is not even and the tray may need to be turned. Once cooked, remove from the oven and let cool a little. Place on a serving plate as a large piece or cut into individual tiles. Using your fingers, distribute the stracciatella, here and there, on top of the pizza. Scatter basil leaves on top and finish with the remaining extra virgin olive oil and some freshly ground pepper.

Serves 6–8

Roman pizza with potato, calamari, spinach and chilli

With a base of potato cooked on this bubbly Roman pizza dough, almost anything will taste good as a topping. Any alternative braised vegetable could just as easily sit here, such as asparagus, artichokes or winter greens.

INGREDIENTS

1 sheet of Roman-style pizza dough
  (see pages 84–88)

500 g (1 lb 2 oz) yellow-fleshed waxy
  potatoes such as Spunta, Nicola
  or Desiree
2 tablespoons extra virgin olive oil
Sea salt and freshly ground black pepper

CALAMARI, SPINACH AND CHILLI

300 g (10½ oz) English spinach,
  washed well
2 French shallots, thinly sliced
2 garlic cloves, crushed
2 red chillies, sliced
3 tablespoons extra virgin olive oil
800 g (1 lb 12 oz) cleaned calamari
  (squid), patted dry and thinly sliced
Sea salt and freshly ground black pepper

METHOD

FOR THE CALAMARI, SPINACH AND CHILLI / Bring a pot of salted water to the boil and plunge in the spinach. Submerge the spinach in the boiling water carefully with a wooden spoon. Boil for 2 minutes, then drain and let it cool. Once cool, wring the spinach well with your hands to remove as much water as possible. Place the spinach on a board and chop roughly. Fry the shallots, garlic and chillies in 2 tablespoons of the olive oil until soft. Add the spinach and stir for 3 minutes, then remove from the heat. In another pan, heat the remaining olive oil on a high flame and fry the calamari for 30–40 seconds, stirring constantly. Add it to the spinach, season with salt and pepper and mix well. Let it come to room temperature. If there is a lot of liquid, drain it off before using on the pizza. Any left-over calamari can be refrigerated for 3–4 days.

TO ASSEMBLE / Scrub the potatoes so the skins are clean. Place in a pot and cover with water. Cover the pot with a lid and bring to the boil. Turn down to a simmer and keep cooking until the potatoes are soft. A skewer should easily pierce the potatoes all the way to the centre. Remove from the heat and drain, letting the potatoes cool. Peel the potatoes and break the flesh apart with your fingers. Place in a bowl and mix with the extra virgin olive oil and the salt and pepper. Preheat the oven to 220°C (425°F). Spread the potatoes on top of the sheet of pizza as evenly as possible. If the dough has risen excessively, press down gently with the tips of your fingers to make small indentations. Bake in the oven for 25 minutes. If the teglia is browning more on one side, your oven is not even and the tray may need to be turned. Once cooked, remove from the oven and let cool a little. Place on a serving plate as a large piece or cut, using scissors, into individual tiles. Distribute the drained calamari, spinach and chilli mixture evenly over the potatoes.

Serves 6–8

Roman pizza with scallops and potato, roast garlic and anchovy dressing

With the addition of chopped anchovies mixed into the roast garlic dressing, this paste turns into a seasoning. Potato and scallops are both sweet and rich, and the garlic and anchovy dressing adds the salty tang.

INGREDIENTS

1 sheet of Roman-style pizza dough
(see pages 84–88)

500 g (1 lb 2 oz) yellow-fleshed waxy
potatoes, such as Spunta, Nicola
or Desiree
2 tablespoons extra virgin olive oil, plus
extra to cook scallops
Sea salt and freshly ground black pepper
24 scallops

ROAST GARLIC AND
ANCHOVY DRESSING
6 whole bulbs of garlic
150–200 g (5½–7 oz) anchovy fillets,
drained of oil
3 tablespoons extra virgin olive oil
Sea salt and freshly ground black pepper

METHOD

FOR THE ROAST GARLIC AND ANCHOVY DRESSING / Preheat the oven to 150°C (300°F). Place the garlic bulbs on a baking tray and roast in the oven until they are soft and creamy inside. This should take 20–30 minutes. Allow to cool, then slice the bulbs in half, across the cloves, and squeeze the garlic out like toothpaste and into the bowl of a food processor. Add the anchovies and the olive oil and blend until it is smooth. Add the salt and pepper. Any leftover dressing can be refrigerated for up to a week.

TO ASSEMBLE / Scrub the potatoes so the skins are clean. Place in a pot and cover with water. Cover the pot with a lid and bring to the boil. Turn down to a simmer and keep cooking until the potatoes are soft. A skewer should easily pierce the potatoes all the way to the centre. Remove from the heat and drain, letting the potatoes cool. Peel the potatoes and break the flesh apart with your fingers. Place in a bowl and mix with the extra virgin olive oil and some salt and pepper. Preheat the oven to 220°C (425°F). Spread the potatoes on top of the sheet of pizza as evenly as possible. If the dough has risen excessively, press down gently with the tips of your fingers to make small indentations. Bake in the oven for 25 minutes. If the teglia is browning more on one side, your oven is not even and the tray may need to be turned. Once cooked, remove from the oven and let cool a little. Heat 2 tablespoons of olive oil in a large heavy-based frying pan. When it is just about to smoke, carefully add the scallops and fry for 15–20 seconds on each side. You may need to do this in three or four lots depending on your pan. Remove the scallops from the pan and place on a tray with paper towel to drain. Place the teglia on a serving plate as a large piece or cut, using scissors, into individual tiles. Distribute the scallops on top and dress with 8 tablespoons of the roast garlic and anchovy dressing.

Serves 6–8

Roman pizza with roast garlic, tomato and olives

This is such a simple combination of great ingredients. When garlic is roasted it loses much of its aggressive flavour: it is tamed into a smoky, sweet paste that can be used in many preparations.

INGREDIENTS

1 sheet of Roman-style pizza dough
(see pages 84–88)

350 g (12 oz/1⅓ cups) tinned San
Marzano whole peeled tomatoes
1 tablespoon extra virgin olive oil
Pinch of sea salt
16 slices of fior di latte mozzarella

ROAST GARLIC, TOMATO AND OLIVES

4 whole bulbs of garlic
150 g (5½ oz/1 cup) large black olives,
pitted and roughly chopped
500 g (1 lb 2 oz) assorted small tomatoes
– baby roma (plum), yellow teardrop,
cherry, cut in half
1 sprig of fresh thyme
1 sprig of fresh oregano
1 tablespoon chopped fresh parsley
2 tablespoons extra virgin olive oil
1 tablespoon red wine vinegar
Sea salt and freshly ground black pepper

METHOD

FOR THE ROAST GARLIC, TOMATO AND OLIVES / Preheat the oven to 160°C (320°F). Place the whole, unpeeled garlic bulbs on a roasting tray or pan and roast for 20 minutes. When ready, the cloves should be soft. Cool a little until they are comfortable to handle and peel each clove, then cut it in half. Place the peeled cloves in a bowl with the chopped olives and tomato halves. Remove the leaves from the sprigs of thyme and oregano and add to the bowl along with the parsley, olive oil and vinegar. Season with salt and pepper to taste and mix well. Any left-over roast tomatoes can be refrigerated for a week.

TO ASSEMBLE / Preheat the oven to 220°C (425°F). Hand squeeze the tomatoes until they're uniformly mashed and mix in the extra virgin olive oil and a pinch of salt. Spread the tomato mixture on top of the sheet of pizza as evenly as possible. If the dough has risen excessively, press down gently with the tips of your fingers to make small indentations to trap the tomato. Bake in the oven for 25 minutes. If the teglia is browning more on one side, your oven is not even and the tray may need to be turned. Once cooked, remove from the oven and let cool a little. Place on a serving plate as a large piece or cut, using scissors, into individual tiles. Begin to dress the pizza by putting two slices of mozzarella on each tile first. Next, scatter with a tablespoon of the roast garlic, tomato and olive mixture for each tile and finish by sprinkling with some of the dressing left in the bowl.

Serves 6–8

THIS PAGE / Zio Vincenzo and Zia Lina staking the San Marzano plants.

Roman pizza with crab, broad beans and chilli

It depends on the dish and the time of the season whether I double peel broad beans or not. Spring broad beans are tender and even their surrounding skin is edible (and occasionally the pod). It's only when summer temperatures start rising that this skin begins to thicken and become bitter. By that time the beans themselves turn mealy and pale and are best dried to store like other beans. The first peel is to take the outer pod off. The second is to then take the skin from each bean. It is the latter that takes time and many have no patience for this sort of job. If you can't be bothered or broad beans aren't available, tender spring peas work just as well. Certainly leaving broad beans unpeeled gives a dish robust flavour and texture.

INGREDIENTS

1 sheet of Roman-style pizza dough
  (see pages 84–88)

300 g (10½ oz/1¼ cups) tinned San
  Marzano peeled tomatoes
2 tablespoons extra virgin olive oil
Sea salt and freshly ground black pepper
300 g (10½ oz) cooked crabmeat
3 tablespoons small fresh parsley leaves

BROAD BEAN AND CHILLI PUREE

370 g (13 oz/2 cups) 'double-peeled'
  broad beans
125 ml (4 fl oz/½ cup) extra virgin olive oil
2 red chillies, thinly sliced
6 tablespoons freshly squeezed lemon juice
Sea salt and freshly ground black pepper

METHOD

FOR THE BROAD BEAN AND CHILLI PUREE / Plunge the broad beans into boiling, salted water for 2 minutes until soft. Put three-quarters of the cooked, still warm, beans in a bowl with the olive oil and mash them with a fork until roughly puréed. Add the rest of the beans, chilli and lemon juice and season with salt and pepper to taste. Mix gently, keeping the whole broad beans intact.

TO ASSEMBLE / Preheat the oven to 220°C (425°F). Hand squeeze the tomatoes until they're uniformly mashed and mix in a tablespoon of extra virgin olive oil and a pinch of salt. Spread the tomato mixture on top of the pizza sheet as evenly as possible. If the dough has risen excessively, press down gently with the tips of your fingers to make small indentations to trap the tomato. Bake in the oven for 25 minutes. If the teglia is browning more on one side, your oven is not even and the tray may need to be turned. Once cooked, remove from the oven and let cool a little. Place on a serving plate as a large piece or cut into individual tiles. Spread the broad bean and chilli purée evenly over the pizza. Scatter with the crabmeat and then the parsley leaves and sprinkle with the remaining olive oil. Finish with a little freshly ground black pepper.

Serves 6–8

Roman pizza with lentils, cauliflower and two cheeses

Braised lentils with cauliflower and cheese is one of my winter standards. The combination of sweet gruyère and tangy Parmigiano Reggiano is the essential element that binds the lot.

INGREDIENTS

1 sheet of Roman-style pizza dough
   (see pages 84–88)

1 medium-sized head of cauliflower
Sea salt and freshly ground black pepper
150 g (5½ oz/1½ cups) gruyère cheese,
   grated
150 g (5½ oz/1½ cups) parmesan cheese,
   grated
2 tablespoons extra virgin olive oil
3 tablespoons chopped fresh parsley

BRAISED LENTILS

3 tablespoons extra virgin olive oil
½ celery heart, finely chopped
1 small carrot, finely chopped
1 small onion, finely chopped
1 small leek, washed thoroughly and sliced
   into 5 mm (¼ inch) half rounds
1 sprig of fresh rosemary, chopped
1 sprig of fresh thyme, chopped
100 g (3½ oz/½ cup) lentils, washed
150 g (5½ oz/⅔ cup) tinned San
   Marzano whole peeled tomatoes
2 garlic cloves, crushed
30 g (1 oz/1 cup) roughly chopped fresh
   flat-leaf parsley
Sea salt and freshly ground black pepper

METHOD

FOR THE BRAISED LENTILS / In a braising pan, lightly fry the vegetables in the extra virgin olive oil until they soften, without colouring them. Add the chopped rosemary and thyme and continue to fry for a minute, stirring. Add the lentils and stir. Add the tomatoes and enough water to just cover the lentils. Cook for 40–60 minutes until the lentils are tender, adding more water if necessary during cooking. When the lentils are cooked, stir in the crushed garlic, parsley and seasoning. Cool until needed. Any left-over lentils can be refrigerated for up to a week.

TO ASSEMBLE / Poach (or steam) the whole cauliflower in boiling water or a steamer until tender. A skewer, or the point of a sharp knife, should be able to pierce the stalk with only a little resistance. Remove from the water or steamer and set aside to cool, then slice 2 cm (¾ inch) thick slices from top to bottom. Cut into small, bite-sized pieces and place between clean dish towels, patting completely dry. Preheat the oven to 220°C (425°F). Take the sheet of pizza and if the dough has risen excessively, press down gently with the tips of your fingers to make small indentations on the surface of the dough. Spread the cooked cauliflower pieces on top of the dough as evenly as possible. Season with a few pinches of salt and some freshly ground pepper. Mix the cheeses together and sprinkle evenly over the cauliflower. Bake in the oven for 25 minutes. If the teglia is browning more on one side, your oven is not even and the tray may need to be turned. Once cooked, remove from the oven and rest for 2–3 minutes. Place on a serving plate as a large piece or cut into individual tiles. Dollop about a cupful of the heated braised lentils here and there with a spoon and sprinkle with the olive oil. Finish with the chopped parsley.

Serves 6–8

Roman pizza with broccoli, marinated anchovies and capers

These are flavours of southern Italy, where vegetables are given their due respect. The anchovies used are filleted and marinated in a little brine and vinegar – not too much – so their flavours are maintained.

INGREDIENTS

1 sheet of Roman-style pizza dough
(see pages 84–88)

400 g (14 oz) fior di latte mozzarella,
thinly sliced
2 tablespoons grated parmesan cheese
1 teaspoon best-quality dried oregano
40 marinated 'white' anchovies
Confit tomatoes (see page 152)
16 caper leaves (optional)
2 tablespoons extra virgin olive oil

COOKED BROCCOLI

1 kg (2 lb 4 oz) broccoli, trimmed of any
tough stalks
2 tablespoons extra virgin olive oil
Sea salt and freshly ground black pepper

FRIED CAPERS

160 g (5½ oz/1 cup) Sicilian capers,
soaked and desalted (see page 36)
250 ml (9 fl oz/1 cup) extra virgin olive oil

METHOD

COOKED BROCCOLI / Bring a large pot, two-thirds filled with water, to the boil. Plunge in the broccoli and cook for 5 minutes. Drain and let the broccoli cool. Chop roughly and place in a bowl. Add the olive oil and season to taste with salt and pepper. Any left-over broccoli can be refrigerated for up to a week.

FOR THE FRIED CAPERS / Dry the capers by patting with a paper towel. Place 1 cm (½ inch) olive oil in the smallest saucepan you can find so you'll use as little oil as possible. Heat until the oil begins to move on its surface. Test by adding a caper. If it sizzles and fries, the oil's hot enough. Add the capers in two batches, frying for 30 seconds, then remove with a slotted spoon to a plate lined with paper towel. These will last for a few days on paper towel in a covered container.

TO ASSEMBLE / Preheat the oven to 220°C (425°F). Take the sheet of pizza and if the dough has risen excessively, press down gently with the tips of your fingers to make small indentations. Distribute the mozzarella on top of the dough as evenly as possible. Sprinkle with the parmesan and oregano. Evenly spread about three-quarters of the cooked broccoli on top and bake in the oven for 25 minutes. If the teglia is browning more on one side, your oven is not even and the tray may need to be turned. Once cooked, remove from the oven and let cool a little. Place on a serving plate as a large piece or cut into individual tiles. Distribute the anchovies, then the fried capers, confit tomatoes and finally the caper leaves on top. Finish with extra virgin olive oil.

Serves 6–8

ED
D&
PIZZE

We know how cleverly inventive the Neapolitans are and the pizza permutations in this chapter are derived from their traditions. You can imagine that the classic filled pizza, the calzone, came about by simply folding the round pizza dough in half, enclosing the ingredients and then sealing its edges before placing it in a wood-fired oven to cook like normal pizza. And you can imagine that a sweet pizza is a natural extension of the savoury. But it is the fried pizza that has captured the imagination of the people of Naples. What began as a necessity after the Second World War (when the costs of fior di latte mozzarella and running wood-fired ovens became greater than frying the same dough filled with ricotta, tomato and pork ciccioli) has continued to delight the city and gain in popularity. The fried pizza has travelled north, all the way to Milan, and I'm certain its popularity will continue to spread worldwide.

Classic calzone

Literally translated, a calzone is a big sock. It's the classic Neapolitan filled pizza. Once you've mastered the method of folding and cooking, you can fill it with your own ingredients. Remember not to fill it too much.

INGREDIENTS

250 g (9 oz) ball of basic pizza dough
    (see pages 74–77), shaped as
    you would a normal round pizza
    (see pages 80–83)
100 g (3½ oz/½ cup) ricotta cheese
100 g (3½ oz) salame napoletano, sliced
    and then cut into strips
80 g (3 oz) fior di latte mozzarella,
    cut into 1 cm (½ inch) cubes, plus
    6 thin slices
3–4 good pinches of freshly ground
    black pepper
1 tablespoon extra virgin olive oil
4 tablespoons tinned San Marzano whole
    peeled tomatoes, puréed

METHOD

TO ASSEMBLE / Place a large tile in your oven for the pizza, then preheat to full heat (without using any fan-forced function) for at least 20 minutes (see page 89). Spread the ricotta gently on half of the dough surface, keeping about 2 cm (¾ inch) from the edges. Scatter salame strips on top and then the cubes of mozzarella. I don't add salt because the salame is salty already. Instead, add the pepper and finally drizzle over the olive oil. Fold the dough over, making a half-moon shape. Press the edges together to seal. Now make a 3 cm (1¼ inch) diameter hole in the dough on the very top, in the middle of the calzone. This will allow steam to escape while the calzone is cooking.

Spoon the tomato in a thin layer over the top of the calzone and place the mozzarella slices along. Place the pizza in the oven for 3–5 minutes until cooked, turning to get an even colour. Remove once cooked.

Makes one 30 cm (12 inch) long calzone

Peking duck roll

This is a filled pizza roll of Peking duck, fior di latte mozzarella, cucumber, ricotta, spring onions and home-made plum sauce devised by Pizzaperta chef Gianluca Donzelli to celebrate Chinese New Year. Chinese barbecued duck is available in just about any city that has Chinese restaurants. This roll works well if passed around in slices as a snack or as a first or second course in its own right.

INGREDIENTS

250 g (9 oz) ball of basic pizza dough (see pages 74–77), shaped as you would a normal round pizza, but make it larger by not leaving a cornice on the edge (see pages 80–83)

80 g (3 oz) fior di latte mozzarella, cut into thin slices

1 small cucumber, cut into long batons about 5 mm (¼ inch) thick

150 g (5½ oz/1 cup) shredded Chinese barbecued duck

3 tablespoons sliced spring onions (scallions)

60 g (2 oz/¼ cup) ricotta cheese

BLOOD PLUM JAM

1.2 kg (2 lb 10 oz) blood plums (or other red-fleshed varieties)

800 g (1 lb 12 oz) sugar

Juice of 1 lemon, strained

1 star anise

2 cm (¾ inch) piece of cinnamon

METHOD

FOR THE BLOOD PLUM JAM / Wash the plums, remove any stalks and dry them well. Cut each plum in half, removing the seed. Put the plum cheeks in a large bowl and mix well with the sugar, lemon juice, star anise and cinnamon. Cover and leave for 2 hours. Put everything into a large saucepan. Bring to the boil, turn down to a simmer and keep simmering for 5 minutes. Return the contents carefully to the bowl, cover and refrigerate overnight. The next day, sieve the liquid into a large saucepan (keeping the plums separate but discarding the star anise and cinnamon) and bring to the boil. Using a sugar thermometer, bring the liquid to 105°C (220°F). Add the plums and keep simmering gently for 10 minutes. Skim any scum that forms on the surface. Place the hot jam into sterilised preserving jars and seal. This makes about 1.5 kg (3 lb 5 oz) jam and can be stored for at least 2 months in a cool place or refrigerator.

TO ASSEMBLE / Place a large tile in your oven for the pizza, then preheat to full heat (without using any fan-forced function) for at least 20 minutes (see page 89). Cut the top and bottom of the pizza base and a little from the sides, leaving a rectangle. Place the slices of mozzarella across the middle of the rectangle. Place the cucumber along in one line, then the duck meat. Finally, scatter over 2 tablespoons of the sliced spring onion. Fold the dough over the filling forming as tight a roll as you can and seal by pinching the edge gently. Place the pizza in the oven for 3–5 minutes until cooked, turning to get an even colour. Remove once cooked and place on a chopping board. Cut into six to eight pieces (you may have to discard the very ends to make the rolls uniform). Place on a serving plate. Put a dollop of ricotta on top of each piece then, using a piping bag, pipe a little of the plum sauce over the top. Finally, garnish with the remaining sliced spring onions.

Makes 6–8 slices

Fried pizza margherita

This is a good snack to prepare if there's some left-over pizza dough. You'll notice that I recommend deep-frying in extra virgin olive oil. If you prefer to use something else, such as a seed oil like peanut or sunflower oil, go ahead. But before you do, please read what I have to say about extra virgin olive oil on page 36.

INGREDIENTS

250g (9 oz) ball of left-over basic pizza
   dough (see pages 74–77)

1 tinned San Marzano whole
   peeled tomato
3 tablespoons extra virgin olive oil
Sea salt
500 ml (17 fl oz/2 cups) extra virgin olive
   oil, for frying (see page 36)
200 g (7 oz) mozzarella, either fior di latte
   or buffalo, torn
12 fresh basil sprigs
100 g (3½ oz/1 cup) finely grated
   parmesan cheese

METHOD

TO ASSEMBLE / Using your hands, a fork or a stick blender, purée the tomato in a bowl and add the olive oil. Mix in a couple of pinches of salt, to taste, until all are well incorporated. Set aside.

Roll the dough into a long sausage – about 3 cm (1¼ inches) thick – on a lightly floured work surface and cut into around 12 gnocchi-shaped pieces. Heat the olive oil in a pot or deep-fryer to 175°C (350°F). Once at that temperature, place the dough pieces carefully in one at a time and fry until crisp and golden. They may need to be turned or moved. Remove with a slotted spoon or strainer and drain on paper towel for 15–20 seconds. Arrange on a serving plate and top each one with a little tomato and a small piece of mozzarella as well as a basil sprig. Sprinkle the grated parmesan on top and serve immediately.

Serves 4 as a snack

Struffoli

This festive Neapolitan Christmas treat is easy to make at any time of year. It's usually formed as little balls, but these irregular shapes are easier to eat with your fingers.

INGREDIENTS

250 g (9 oz) ball of basic pizza dough
    (see pages 74–77)

500 ml (17 fl oz/2 cups) extra virgin olive
    oil, for frying (see page 36)
175 g (6 oz/½ cup) honey
1 tablespoon grated lemon zest
1 tablespoon grated orange zest
2 tablespoons white sugar confetti
1 tablespoon chopped candied
    cedro (citron)

METHOD

TO ASSEMBLE / Roll the dough into a long sausage – about 2 cm (¾ inch) thick – on a lightly floured work surface and cut into around 12 pieces, each about 5 cm (2 inches) long. Heat the olive oil in a pot or deep-fryer to 175°C (350°F). Once at that temperature, place the dough pieces carefully in one at a time and fry until crisp and golden. They may need to be turned or moved. Remove with a slotted spoon or strainer and drain on paper towel.

While the struffoli are draining, heat the honey over a medium heat, in a small saucepan, until it's very liquid and runny. Using a spoon, drizzle the honey over the struffoli to coat them well. Sprinkle with lemon and orange zest and top with the sugar confetti and candied cedro.

Serves 4

Fried pizza with scarola and crabmeat

The idea for this fried pizza came from a dish by Enzo Coccia, who devised it after reading Ippolito Cavalcanti's 1837 manuscript Cucina Teorico-Pratica. *Scarola is an endive (Cichorium endivia), which is harvested in autumn through to early spring. It's popular in Italy either raw or cooked. This recipe is for two fried pizze, but it's always best to make a lot more while the oil is hot.*

INGREDIENTS

250 g (9 oz) ball of basic pizza dough
    (see pages 74–77)

160 g (5½ oz) cooked crabmeat
1 teaspoon colatura d'alici
Extra virgin olive oil or peanut oil, for frying

FRIED SCAROLA
3–4 heads of scarola, washed well
2 tablespoons extra virgin olive oil
1 garlic clove, crushed
10 Gaeta (or similar) black olives, pitted
    and quartered
2 tablespoons sultanas (golden raisins)
60 ml (2 fl oz/¼ cup) dry white wine
3 tablespoons toasted pine nuts
Sea salt and freshly ground black pepper

METHOD

FOR THE FRIED SCAROLA / Divide the scarola into individual leaves. Heat the olive oil in a wide frying pan and lightly fry the garlic and olives for a minute, making sure the garlic does not colour. Add the scarola leaves and sultanas and mix for 30 seconds until the leaves have softened a little. Add the wine and turn up the heat, letting the liquid evaporate. Cover the pan, turn down the heat to low and cook for 2–3 minutes. Remove the lid, add the toasted pine nuts, season with salt and pepper to taste, mix and cook off any liquid that has formed. Remove from the heat and let it cool completely before using for the fried pizza. This makes enough for 8–10 fried pizze.

TO ASSEMBLE / Divide the dough ball in two. Prepare the pizza discs as you would for normal pizza, on a lightly floured surface, but make the discs around 16–18 cm (6–7 inches) wide and don't leave the cornice on the border (see pages 80–83). As the discs are going to be folded in half, divide about a quarter of the fried scarola mixture evenly between the bottom half of each disc and spread it out to about 3 cm (1¼ inches) from the bottom and 5–6 cm (2–2½ inches) from the sides. Scatter the crabmeat on top and season with ½ teaspoon of colatura d'alici sprinkled on each. Fold each disc to enclose the stuffing and lightly pinch the borders to seal them. Choose a pot or deep-fryer that is wide enough to contain the stuffed pizza. The amount of oil will depend on the pot used: you need oil at a depth of at least 4–5 cm (1½–2 inches). Heat the oil to 175°C (350°F). Once the oil is at that temperature, place the pizze carefully in, one at a time, and fry until crisp and golden. They will need to be moved constantly and turned so that they are golden on both sides. Remove with a slotted spoon or 'spider' and drain on paper towel. Serve hot.

Makes 2 fried pizze

THIS PAGE / Eating pizza fritta on the streets of Naples. **OPPOSITE** / Pizza fritta at Zia Esterina Sorbillo in the heart of Naples.

Fried pizza with pork belly, ricotta and provola

This classic fried pizza is usually made with cicoli, the left-over rendered fatty parts of a pig. Once the fat had been rendered out to be used as a cooking medium called sugno (a type of dripping), the left-over solid is chopped up as cicoli. I have used roast pork belly instead.

INGREDIENTS

250 g (9 oz) ball of basic pizza dough
(see pages 74–77)

230 g (8 oz/1 cup) ricotta cheese
200 g (7 oz) slow-roasted pork belly (see
page 176)
Sea salt and freshly ground black pepper
4 fresh basil leaves
150 g (5½ oz/1½ cups) coarsely grated
provola cheese
Extra virgin olive oil or peanut oil, for frying

METHOD

TO ASSEMBLE / Divide the dough ball in two. Prepare the pizza discs as you would for normal pizze, on a lightly floured surface, but make the discs around 16–18 cm (6–7 inches) wide and don't leave the cornice on the border (see pages 80–83). As the discs are going to be folded in half, spread the ricotta evenly on the bottom half of each disc and spread it out to about 3 cm (1¼ inches) from the bottom and 5–6 cm (2–2½ inches) from the sides. Cut the pork belly into 5 mm (¼ inch) cubes and place on top of the ricotta. Season with a little salt and pepper. Place two basil leaves on top of each and cover with the provola cheese. Fold each disc to enclose the stuffing and lightly pinch the borders to seal them. Choose a pot or fryer that is wide enough to contain the stuffed pizza. The amount of oil will depend on the pot used: you need oil at a depth of at least 4–5 cm (1½–2 inches). Heat the oil to 175°C (350°F). Once the oil is at that temperature, place the pizze carefully in, one at a time, and fry until crisp and golden. They will need to be moved constantly and turned so that they are golden on both sides. Remove with a slotted spoon or 'spider' and drain on paper towel. Serve hot.

Makes 2 fried pizze

Rio – banana and macadamia sweet calzone

This is a filled dessert pizza devised by Pizzaperta chef Gianluca Donzelli to commemorate the Brazil leg of the World Surf League: The Rio Pro.

INGREDIENTS

250 g (9 oz) ball of basic pizza dough (see pages 74–77), shaped as you would a normal round pizza (see pages 80–83)

40 g (1½ oz/¼ cup) ricotta cheese
50 g (1¾ oz/⅓ cup) 70% cocoa dark chocolate buttons
1 large banana, halved lengthways
1 tablespoon guava jam
1 tablespoon icing (confectioners') sugar, for dusting
1 tablespoon amarena cherries or other berry coulis

MACADAMIA BRITTLE

170 g (6 oz/1⅓ cups) shelled, unsalted macadamia pieces
270 g (9½ oz/1¼ cups) sugar
60 ml (2 fl oz/¼ cup) water
60 ml (2 fl oz/¼ cup) light corn syrup
35 g (1¼ oz/2 tablespoons) unsalted butter
½ teaspoon baking powder
Pinch of sea salt

METHOD

FOR THE MACADAMIA BRITTLE / Place the shelled, unsalted macadamias on a baking tray and roast in a preheated 180°C (350°F) oven for about 10–12 minutes. Allow the nuts to cool. In a saucepan combine the sugar, water, corn syrup and butter. Cook over a medium heat until the mixture is a light caramel colour. Remove from the heat and quickly whisk in the baking powder, salt and the macadamia nuts. With a buttered spatula, spread the mixture quickly onto a non-stick baking sheet. Cool completely. Break into shards or grind in a mortar and pestle or food processor to make praline. The brittle can be stored in an airtight container between sheets of baking paper for up to 2 weeks.

TO ASSEMBLE / Place a large tile in your oven for the pizza, then preheat to full heat (without using any fan-forced function) for at least 20 minutes (see page 89). Spread the ricotta on one half of the dough circle, remembering that it will be folded over and sealed into a crescent shape. Scatter the buttons over the ricotta, then place the two banana halves on top. Fold the dough over the filling, forming a crescent shape, and seal by pinching the edge gently. Place the pizza in the oven for 3–5 minutes until cooked, turning to get an even colour. Once cooked, remove from the oven and place on a chopping board. Cut into four pieces. Place on a serving plate. Put a little guava jam on top of each piece, dust with icing sugar, scatter over 1 tablespoon of the crushed macadamia brittle and finish by drizzling on the berry coulis.

Serves 4

Pillow of dreams

Italians love their Nutella. It's a treat given to them in their childhood and many continue this love affair when they become adults. Nutella is now famous throughout the world, but its origins begin with Italian pastry maker, Pietro Ferrero, who created a chocolate bar cut with high-quality Piemontese hazelnut paste. That was in 1946 when chocolate was in short supply post-war. It became an instant success. Many loved having bread and chocolate for breakfast, so in 1951 a version with a creamy, spreadable consistency was invented called Supercrema. It was Pietro's son Michele who rebranded it as Nutella in 1963 and it is now enjoyed by millions of people all over the world. This is Pizzaperta's version of a Nutella pizza. When our chef, Gianluca Donzelli, created it he said it was 'like a dream'. 'A pillow of dreams,' I said. Indeed it is.

INGREDIENTS

250 g (9 oz) ball of basic pizza dough (see pages 74–77), shaped as you would a normal round pizza, but make it larger by not leaving a cornice on the edge (see pages 80–83)

4 tablespoons Nutella
2 tablespoons flaked almonds
Icing (confectioners') sugar, for dusting
1 scoop of vanilla gelato
2 strawberries, halved
1 tablespoon thinly sliced fresh mint leaves
1 sprig of fresh mint

METHOD

TO ASSEMBLE / Place a large tile in your oven for the pizza, then preheat to full heat (without using any fan-forced function) for at least 20 minutes (see page 89). Cut the pizza base into as large a square as possible. Place a tablespoon of Nutella halfway between each corner and the middle of the square. Scatter the flaked almonds on top of each tablespoon of Nutella. Fold each of the corners of the dough into the centre over the filling, forming a smaller square, and seal by pinching the edges gently where the folds meet. Place the pizza in the oven for 3–5 minutes until cooked, turning to get an even colour. Once cooked, remove from the oven and place on a board. Sprinkle with a light dusting of icing sugar. Place on a serving plate. Add a scoop of vanilla gelato in the middle, a strawberry half in each corner and scatter the sliced mint on top. Finish with a mint sprig on the gelato.

Serves 4

Index

Page numbers in bold indicate photographs.

Agrigenus 24
Altamura **139, 199**
anchovies
    about 28–33, 29, 30, 31
    Pizza rossa: Sicilian capers and anchovies 102
    Roman pizza with broccoli, marinated
        anchovies and capers 214
    Roman pizza with scallops and potato,
        roast garlic and anchovy dressing 207
    Roman pizza with tuna tartare 180
    Roman pizza with vitello tonnato 170
    Salsa verde 166
    Tuna tartare 180
    Vitello tonnato 170
artichokes
    Pizza bianca: pork and fennel sausage,
        artichoke, buffalo ricotta 142
asparagus
    Pizza bianca: Montasio, broccoli and
        prosciutto crackle 132
    Pizza rossa: chargrilled vegetables 98
Associazione Verace Pizza Napoletana 8
avocado
    Pizza bianca: frutti di mare and avocado 118

Baba ganoush 190
baking pizza
    in domestic oven 89
    in wood-fired oven 89
balsamic vinegar
    about 160
    Roman pizza with figs, prosciutto and
        balsamic 160
Banana and macadamia sweet calzone 234
basil
    Fried pizza margherita 224
    Pizza alla procidana 46
    Pizza Capitanata 52

Pizza rossa: Margherita 96
Roman pizza margherita 186
Roman pizza with eggplant parmigiana 172
Roman pizza with tomato and stracciatella 204
San Marzano sauce 172
beans
    Pizza rossa: chargrilled vegetables 98
beef
    Braised peppered beef cheeks 202
    Roman pizza with potato and braised beef
        cheeks 202
    Roman pizza with roast beef, shiitake and
        grana 192
    beef tongue
    Roman pizza with grilled ox tongue,
        parsnip purée, salsa verde 166
beetroot
    Pizza bianca: beetroot, onion and roast garlic
        138
Bonci, Gabriele 58–9, 62
broad beans
    about 210
    Broad bean and chilli purée 210
    Roman pizza with crab, broad beans and
        chilli 210
broccoli
    Broccoli cream 132
    Pan-fried broccoli 196
    Pizza bianca: Montasio, broccoli and
        prosciutto crackle 132
    Roman pizza with broccoli, marinated
        anchovies and capers 214
    Roman pizza with cuttlefish, broccoli and
        chilli 196
buffalo mozzarella 24–5, **24, 26, 27**
burrata
    about 28
    Pizza bianca: lucariello, onion confettura
        and burrata 137

Pizza Capitanata 52
Roman pizza with prosciutto, burrata and
    eggplant 158

calamari
    Pizza bianca: frutti di mare and avocado 118
    Pizza rossa: calamari, chilli and ginger
        108
    Roman pizza with potato, calamari,
        spinach and chilli 206
calzone 11, 220
capers
    about 36–7
    Caper and olive dressing 162
    Fried capers 214
    Pizza bianca: pickled lettuce, capers, olives
        and tomatoes 152
    Pizza rossa: Sicilian capers and anchovies 102
    Pizza rossa: tuna, Mediterranean herbs and
        colatura 106
    Roman pizza with broccoli, marinated
        anchovies and capers 214
    Roman pizza with octopus and potato 162
    Roman pizza with tuna tartare 180
    Roman pizza with vitello tonnato 170
    Salsa verde 166
    Tuna tartare 180
    Vitello tonnato 170
capocollo
    about 33, **33, 34–5**
    Pizza bianca: capocollo and fennel 122
    Pizza bianca: capocollo, pickled red onion
        and pecorino 150
capsicums
    Pizza bianca: hot calabrese 116
    Pizza: 'nduja, fior di latte mozzarella, long
        chillies and goat's cheese 68
Caramia, Piero 33

La Cascina dei Sapori 66–7
Caseificio Olanda 28
cauliflower
    Roman pizza with lentils, cauliflower and
        two cheeses 212
cavolo nero
    Cavolo nero frittata 174
    Roman pizza filled with cavolo nero frittata
        and 'nduja 174
    Roman pizza with cavolo nero, mushrooms
        and lardo 194
Cetara 101, **128–9, 181**
chestnuts
    Chestnut purée 164
    Roman pizza with roast duck, chestnuts and
        mushrooms 164
chickpeas
    Chickpea purée 120
    Pizza bianca: chickpeas, eggplant and
        salted ricotta 120
chicory
    Cooked chicory 124
    Pizza bianca: chicory, salame and
        stracciatella 124
chillies
    Broad bean and chilli purée 210
    Pizza Capitanata 52
    Pizza rossa: calamari, chilli and ginger 108
    Roman pizza with crab, broad beans and
        chilli 210
chocolate
    Banana and macadamia sweet calzone 234
    Nutella 236
    Pillow of dreams 236
cicoli 232
Coccia, Enzo 10, 42–3, 46
codification of pizza 10
colatura
    about 28, 29, 30, 31
    Pizza rossa: tuna, Mediterranean herbs and
        colatura 106
crab
    Fried pizza with scarola and crabmeat 228
    Roman pizza with crab, broad beans and
        chilli 210

cuttlefish
    Roman pizza with cuttlefish, broccoli and
        chilli 196

Danicoop 21
desserts & sweets
    Banana and macadamia sweet calzone 234
    Macadamia brittle 234
    Pillow of dreams 236
    Struffoli 226
domestic oven cooking 89
Donzelli, Gianluca 234, 236
duck
    Peking duck roll 222
    Roast duck breast 164
    Roman pizza with roast duck, chestnuts and
        mushrooms 164

Eduardo, Zio 20, 23
eggplant
    Baba ganoush 190
    Pizza bianca: chickpeas, eggplant and
        salted ricotta 120
    Pizza rossa: chargrilled vegetables 98
    Roman pizza with baba ganoush and
        prawns 190
    Roman pizza with eggplant parmigiana 172
    Roman pizza with prosciutto, burrata and
        eggplant 158
eggs
    Cavolo nero frittata 174
    Roman pizza filled with cavolo nero frittata
        and 'nduja 174
endive, *see* scarola

fennel
    Pizza bianca: capocollo and fennel 122
    Pizza bianca: pork and fennel sausage,
        artichoke, buffalo ricotta 142
Ferrero, Pietro 236
figs
    Fig jam 176

Roman pizza with figs, prosciutto and
    balsamic 160
Roman pizza with gorgonzola and figs 193
Roman pizza with pork belly, pickled onion
    and fig jam 176
fior de latte mozzarella 25, 28
flour 7, 10, 14, 15–18, 73
focaccia 11, 12
fontina
    Pizza bianca: black truffle and fontina 148
    Roman pizza with silverbeet, field
        mushrooms and fontina 178
Forno Antico Santa Chiara 11, 11, 12
fried pizza, history of 219
Fried pizza with pork belly, ricotta and
    provola 232
Fried pizza with scarola and crabmeat 228
friggitelli
    Pizza: 'nduja, fior di latte mozzarella, long
        chillies and goat's cheese 68
frittata 174

garlic
    Pizza alla procidana 46
    Pizza bianca: beetroot, onion and roast
        garlic 138
    Roast garlic dressing 138
    Roast garlic, tomato and olives 208
    Roman pizza with roast garlic, tomato and
        olives 208
    Roman pizza with scallops and potato,
        roast garlic and anchovy dressing 207
    Salsa verde 166
ginger
    Pizza rossa: calamari, chilli and ginger 108
Giordano, Giulio 28
goat's cheese
    Pizza: drunken pears, ash-rind goat's cheese 56
    Pizza: 'nduja, fior di latte mozzarella, long
        chillies and goat's cheese 68
Goldman Fowler, Amy 21
gorgonzola
    Pizza bianca: gorgonzola, potato and
        radicchio 130

Pizza bianca: quattro formaggi and walnuts
140
Roman pizza with gorgonzola and figs 193
Grana Padano
Pumpkin purée 136
gruyère
Roman pizza with lentils, cauliflower and
two cheeses 212

ham
Pizza rossa: smoked leg ham, mushroom
and sage 104
hazelnuts
Roman pizza with ricotta, persimmons and
'nduja 62
history of pizza 7, 8–11
'new wave' pizza movement 7, 11
honey
Pizza: drunken pears, ash-rind goat's
cheese 56
Struffoli 226

I Tigli 55

jam
Blood plum jam 222
Fig jam 176

La Cascina dei Sapori 66–7
lamb
Pizza bianca: lamb belly, ricotta and
Mediterranean herbs 146
Slow-cooked lamb belly 146
lardo
Roman pizza with cavolo nero, mushrooms
and lardo 194
leeks
Cavolo nero frittata 174
Pizza rossa: chargrilled vegetables 98
Roman pizza filled with cavolo nero frittata
and 'nduja 174

lentils
Braised lentils 212
Roman pizza with lentils, cauliflower and
two cheeses 212
lettuce
Pickled lettuce 152
Pizza bianca: pickled lettuce, capers, olives
and tomatoes 152
lievito madre, see sourdough starter
Lina, Zia **209**

macadamias
Banana and macadamia sweet calzone
234
Macadamia brittle 234
Macella, Vito 11, 11, 12
margherita, Fried pizza 224
margherita, Roman pizza 186
marinara pizza
misconceptions of 118
Pizza rossa: marinara Napoletana 94
Mattozzi, Antonio 8, 10
mint
Pizza bianca: prawns, zucchini and mint 114
Montasio
Pizza bianca: Montasio, broccoli and
prosciutto crackle 132
mozzarella
about 24–28, 24, 26, 27
Classic calzone 220
Fried pizza margherita 224
Peking duck roll 222
Pizza bianca: beetroot, onion and roast
garlic 138
Pizza bianca: capocollo and fennel 122
Pizza bianca: capocollo, pickled red onion
and pecorino 150
Pizza bianca: chickpeas, eggplant and
salted ricotta 120
Pizza bianca: chicory, salame and
stracciatella 124
Pizza bianca: frutti di mare and avocado 118
Pizza bianca: gorgonzola, potato and
radicchio 130

Pizza bianca: lamb belly, ricotta and
Mediterranean herbs 146
Pizza bianca: Montasio, broccoli and
prosciutto crackle 132
Pizza bianca: pancetta, wilted rucola and
taleggio 126
Pizza bianca: pickled lettuce, capers, olives
and tomatoes 152
Pizza bianca: pork and fennel sausage,
artichoke, buffalo ricotta 142
Pizza bianca: prawns, zucchini and mint 114
Pizza bianca: prosciutto and bufala 134
Pizza bianca: quattro formaggi and walnuts 140
Pizza: drunken pears, ash-rind goat's
cheese 56
Pizza: 'nduja, fior di latte mozzarella, long
chillies and goat's cheese 68
Pizza rossa: calamari, chilli and ginger 108
Pizza rossa: chargrilled vegetables 98
Pizza rossa: Margherita 96
Pizza rossa: Sicilian capers and anchovies 102
Pizza rossa: smoked leg ham, mushroom
and sage 104
Pizza rossa: tuna, Mediterranean herbs and
colatura 106
Roman pizza margherita 186
Roman pizza with broccoli, marinated
anchovies and capers 214
Roman pizza with eggplant parmigiana 172
Roman pizza with pork belly, pickled onion
and fig jam 176
Roman pizza with roast garlic, tomato and
olives 208
Roman pizza with zucchini trifolati 188
mushrooms
Braised mushrooms 164
Pan-fried field mushrooms 178
Pizza rossa: smoked leg ham, mushroom
and sage 104
Roman pizza with cavolo nero, mushrooms
and lardo 194
Roman pizza with roast beef, shiitake and
grana 192
Roman pizza with roast duck, chestnuts and
mushrooms 164

Roman pizza with silverbeet, field
mushrooms and fontina 178
mustard fruit
Pumpkin purée 136

'nduja
Pizza bianca: hot calabrese 116
Pizza: 'nduja, fior di latte mozzarella, long
chillies and goat's cheese 68
Roman pizza filled with cavolo nero frittata
and 'nduja 174
Roman pizza with ricotta, persimmons
and 'nduja 62
Neapolitan pizza, codification of 10
'new wave' pizza movement 7, 11
Nutella
origins of 236
Pillow of dreams 236

octopus **109**
Roman pizza with octopus and potato 162
Slow-cooked octopus 162
olive oil 14, 19, 36
olives
about 33, 36
Caper and olive dressing 162
Fried pizza with scarola and crabmeat 228
Pizza bianca: hot calabrese 116
Pizza bianca: pickled lettuce, capers, olives
and tomatoes 152
Pizza bianca: pumpkin, scamorza and
zucchini flowers 136
Pizza rossa: Sicilian capers and anchovies
102
Pizza rossa: tuna, Mediterranean herbs and
colatura 106
Roast garlic, tomato and olives 208
Roman pizza with octopus and potato 162
Roman pizza with roast garlic, tomato and
olives 208
onions
Onion confettura 137
Pickled red onion 150

Pizza bianca: capocollo, pickled red onion
and pecorino 150
Pizza bianca: lucariello, onion confettura
and burrata 137
Pizza Capitanata 52
Roman pizza with pork belly, pickled onion
and fig jam 176
Roman pizza with red onion 200
Slow-cooked onion 52
oregano 37
ox tongue
Roman pizza with grilled ox tongue,
parsnip purée, salsa verde 166

Padoan, Simone 54–5, 56
pancetta
Pizza bianca: pancetta, wilted rucola and
taleggio 126
Pappalardo, Antonio 66–7, 68
parmesan
Cavolo nero frittata 174
Pizza bianca: black truffle and fontina 148
Pizza bianca: lamb belly, ricotta and
Mediterranean herbs 146
Pizza bianca: pickled lettuce, capers, olives
and tomatoes 152
Pizza bianca: pork and fennel sausage,
artichoke, buffalo ricotta 142
Pizza bianca: pumpkin, scamorza and
zucchini flowers 136
Pizza rossa: chargrilled vegetables 98
Roman pizza filled with cavolo nero frittata
and 'nduja 174
Roman pizza with eggplant parmigiana
172
Roman pizza with lentils, cauliflower and
two cheeses 212
Roman pizza with silverbeet, field
mushrooms and fontina 178
parsley
Salsa verde 166
Vitello tonnato 170
parsnips
Parsnip purée 166

Roman pizza with grilled ox tongue,
parsnip purée, salsa verde 166
pears
Pizza: drunken pears, ash-rind goat's cheese 56
pecans
Pizza: drunken pears, ash-rind goat's cheese 56
pecorino
Pizza bianca: capocollo and fennel 122
Pizza bianca: capocollo, pickled red onion
and pecorino 150
Pizza bianca: quattro formaggi and
walnuts 140
Peking duck roll 222
Pere ubriache, caprino alla cenere 56
persimmons
Roman pizza with ricotta, persimmons
and 'nduja 62
Petrini, Carlo 14
pickles
Pickled lettuce 152
Pickled red onion 150
Pillow of dreams 236
pine nuts
Fried pizza with scarola and crabmeat 228
Pizza bianca: chickpeas, eggplant and
salted ricotta 120
Pizza bianca: pumpkin, scamorza and
zucchini flowers 136
Roman pizza with tuna tartare 180
Tuna tartare 180
"pizza a taglio" tradition 59
Pizza alla procidana 46
Pizza bianca: beetroot, onion and roast garlic 138
Pizza bianca: black truffle and fontina 148
Pizza bianca: capocollo and fennel 122
Pizza bianca: capocollo, pickled red onion
and pecorino 150
Pizza bianca: chickpeas, eggplant and salted
ricotta 120
Pizza bianca: chicory, salame and
stracciatella 124
Pizza bianca: frutti di mare (seafood) and
avocado 118
Pizza bianca: gorgonzola, potato and
radicchio 130

Pizza bianca: hot calabrese 116
Pizza bianca: lamb belly, ricotta and Mediterranean herbs 146
Pizza bianca: lucariello, onion confettura and burrata 137
Pizza bianca: Montasio, broccoli and prosciutto crackle 132
Pizza bianca: pancetta, wilted rucola and taleggio 126
Pizza bianca: pickled lettuce, capers, olives and tomatoes 152
Pizza bianca: pork and fennel sausage, artichoke, buffalo ricotta 142
Pizza bianca: prawns, zucchini and mint 114
Pizza bianca: prosciutto and bufala 134
Pizza bianca: pumpkin, scamorza and zucchini flowers 136
Pizza bianca: quattro formaggi and walnuts 140
Pizza Capitanata 52
pizza dough
    cooking 89
    Dried yeast dough 75
    Fresh yeast dough 75
    indirect method 76
    Roman-style basic 84
    Roman-style mixed wheat 85
    shaping into balls 80-81
    shaping into bases 82, 82-83
    shaping Roman-style 86-88
    Sourdough starter 79
    Spelt pizza dough 78
    temperature of 77
Pizzaperta Manfredi 7, 67, 234
Pizzaria La Notizia 42-43
Pizza ricotta, cachi e 'nduja 62
Pizzarium 59
Pizza rossa: calamari, chilli and ginger 108
Pizza rossa: chargrilled vegetables 98
Pizza rossa: Margherita 96
Pizza rossa: marinara Napoletana 94
Pizza rossa: Sicilian capers and anchovies 102
Pizza rossa: smoked leg ham, mushroom and sage 104

Pizza rossa: tuna, Mediterranean herbs and colatura 106
plums
    blood plum jam 222
porcini mushrooms
    Roman pizza with cavolo nero, mushrooms and lardo 194
    Roman pizza with roast duck, chestnuts and mushrooms 164
pork, see also ham, 'nduja, prosciutto, salame, salumi production, sausage
    Fried pizza with pork belly, ricotta and provola 232
    Roman pizza with pork belly, pickled onion and fig jam 176
    Slow-roasted pork belly 176
potatoes
    Pizza bianca: gorgonzola, potato and radicchio 130
    Roman pizza with octopus and potato 162
    Roman pizza with potato and braised beef cheeks 202
    Roman pizza with potato, calamari, spinach and chilli 206
    Roman pizza with scallops and potato, roast garlic and anchovy dressing 207
prawns
    Pizza bianca: frutti di mare and avocado 118
    Pizza bianca: prawns, zucchini and mint 114
    Roman pizza with baba ganoush and prawns 190
Presidio Slow Food 21, 24
prosciutto
    Pizza bianca: Montasio, broccoli and prosciutto crackle 132
    Pizza bianca: prosciutto and bufala 134
    Prosciutto crackle 132
    Roman pizza with figs, prosciutto and balsamic 160
    Roman pizza with prosciutto, burrata and eggplant 158
provola cheese
    Fried pizza with pork belly, ricotta and provola 232

pumpkin
    Pizza bianca: pumpkin, scamorza and zucchini flowers 136
    Pizza rossa: chargrilled vegetables 98
    Pumpkin purée 136
    Pumpkin, scamorza and zucchini flowers 136

radicchio
    Pizza bianca: gorgonzola, potato and radicchio 130
    Roman pizza with vitello tonnato 170
raisins
    Roman pizza with tuna tartare 180
Rea, Patricia 49
Ricci, Patrick 48-49
ricotta
    Banana and macadamia sweet calzone 234
    Classic calzone 220
    Fried pizza with pork belly, ricotta and provola 232
    Pizza bianca: lamb belly, ricotta and Mediterranean herbs 146
    Pizza bianca: pork and fennel sausage, artichoke, buffalo ricotta 142
    Pizza bianca: pumpkin, scamorza and zucchini flowers 136
    Pizza bianca: quattro formaggi and walnuts 140
    Roman pizza with ricotta, persimmons and 'nduja 62
ricotta salata, see salted ricotta
Rio (banana and macadamia sweet calzone) 234
rocket
    Pizza bianca: pancetta, wilted rucola and taleggio 126
    Pizza bianca: prosciutto and bufala 134
    Pizza: drunken pears, ash-rind goat's cheese 56
    Roman pizza filled with cavolo nero frittata and 'nduja 174
    Roman pizza with pork belly, pickled onion and fig jam 176

Roman pizza a taglio tradition 59
Roman pizza filled with cavolo nero frittata
and 'nduja 174
Roman pizza margherita 186
Roman pizza with baba ganoush and
prawns 190
Roman pizza with broccoli, marinated
anchovies and capers 214
Roman pizza with cavolo nero, mushrooms
and lardo 194
Roman pizza with crab, broad beans and
chilli 210
Roman pizza with cuttlefish, broccoli and
chilli 196
Roman pizza with eggplant parmigiana 172
Roman pizza with figs, prosciutto and
balsamic 160
Roman pizza with gorgonzola and figs 193
Roman pizza with grilled ox tongue,
parsnip purée, salsa verde 166
Roman pizza with lentils, cauliflower and
two cheeses 212
Roman pizza with octopus and potato 162
Roman pizza with pork belly, pickled onion
and fig jam 176
Roman pizza with potato and braised beef
cheeks 202
Roman pizza with potato, calamari, spinach
and chilli 206
Roman pizza with prosciutto, burrata and
eggplant 158
Roman pizza with red onion 200
Roman pizza with ricotta, persimmons and
'nduja 62
Roman pizza with roast beef, shiitake and grana
192
Roman pizza with roast duck, chestnuts and
mushrooms 164
Roman pizza with roast garlic, tomato and
olives 208
Roman pizza with scallops and potato, roast
garlic and anchovy dressing 207
Roman pizza with silverbeet, field mushrooms
and fontina 178

Roman pizza with tomato and stracciatella 204
Roman pizza with tuna tartare 180
Roman pizza with vitello tonnato 170
Roman pizza with zucchini trifolati 188
rosemary
Pizza bianca: gorgonzola, potato and
radicchio 130
Rosemary oil 130
Ruggiero, Paolo 21

sage
Pizza rossa: smoked leg ham, mushroom
and sage 104
salame
Classic calzone 220
Pizza bianca: chicory, salame and
stracciatella 124
salt 19
salted ricotta
Pizza bianca: chickpeas, eggplant and
salted ricotta 120
salumi production 33, 34–5
San Marzano tomatoes 21, 24, **22, 23**
Santoro, Giuseppe 33
sausage
Pizza bianca: hot calabrese 116
Pizza bianca: pork and fennel sausage,
artichoke, buffalo ricotta 142
scallops
Pizza bianca: frutti di mare and avocado 118
Roman pizza with scallops and potato,
roast garlic and anchovy dressing 207
scamorza
Roman pizza with eggplant parmigiana 172
scarola
Fried pizza with scarola and crabmeat 228
shiitake mushrooms
Roman pizza with cavolo nero, mushrooms
and lardo 194
Roman pizza with roast beef, shiitake and
grana 192
Roman pizza with roast duck, chestnuts and
mushrooms 164

silverbeet
Braised silverbeet 178
Roman pizza with silverbeet, field
mushrooms and fontina 178
smoked provola cheese
Pizza bianca: hot calabrese 116
smoked scamorza
Pizza alla procidana 46
Pizza bianca: pumpkin, scamorza and
zucchini flowers 136
sourdough starter 19, 79
spinach
Roman pizza with potato, calamari,
spinach and chilli 206
stracciatella
Pizza bianca: chicory, salame and
stracciatella 124
Roman pizza with tomato and stracciatella
204
strawberries
Pillow of dreams 236
Struffoli 226
styles of pizza 10–11, 43
sugno 232
sultanas
Fried pizza with scarola and crabmeat 228
sweets, *see* desserts & sweets

taleggio
Pizza bianca: pancetta, wilted rucola and
taleggio 126
tarragon
Pizza bianca: lucariello, onion confettura
and burrata 137
Terra, Grani, Esplorazioni 49
tomatoes
about 21–4, 93
Braised lentils 212
Confit tomatoes 152
Fried pizza margherita 224
Pizza alla procidana 46
Pizza bianca: chickpeas, eggplant and
salted ricotta 120

Pizza bianca: frutti di mare (seafood) and avocado 118
Pizza bianca: hot calabrese 116
Pizza bianca: lamb belly, ricotta and Mediterranean herbs 146
Pizza bianca: lucariello, onion confettura and burrata 137
Pizza bianca: pickled lettuce, capers, olives and tomatoes 152
Pizza bianca: pork and fennel sausage, artichoke, buffalo ricotta 142
Pizza bianca: prosciutto and bufala 134
Pizza rossa: calamari, chilli and ginger 108
Pizza rossa: chargrilled vegetables 98
Pizza rossa: Margherita 96
Pizza rossa: marinara Napoletana 94
Pizza rossa: Sicilian capers and anchovies 102
Pizza rossa: smoked leg ham, mushroom and sage 104
Pizza rossa: tuna, Mediterranean herbs and colatura 106
Roast cherry tomatoes 134
Roast garlic, tomato and olives 208
Roast tomatoes 46
Roman pizza margherita 186
Roman pizza with baba ganoush and prawns 190
Roman pizza with cavolo nero, mushrooms and lardo 194
Roman pizza with crab, broad beans and chilli 210
Roman pizza with cuttlefish, broccoli and chilli 196
Roman pizza with eggplant parmigiana 172
Roman pizza with roast beef, shiitake and grana 192
Roman pizza with roast garlic, tomato and olives 208
Roman pizza with tomato and stracciatella 204
Roman pizza with zucchini trifolati 188
San Marzano sauce 172
Tomato fillets 142
Yellow tomato passata 52

truffles
    Pizza bianca: black truffle and fontina 148
tuna
    Pizza rossa: tuna, Mediterranean herbs and colatura 106
    Roman pizza with tuna tartare 180
    Roman pizza with vitello tonnato 170
    Tuna tartare 180

Vitello tonnato 170
veal
    Roman pizza with vitello tonnato 170
Vitello tonnato 170
Vincenzo, Zio **209**

walnuts
    Pizza bianca: quattro formaggi and walnuts 140
water (as pizza dough ingredient) 18
wood-fired oven cooking 89

yeast 18–19

Zia Esterina Sorbillo **231**
zucchini
    Pizza bianca: prawns, zucchini and mint 114
    Pizza rossa: chargrilled vegetables 98
    Roman pizza with zucchini trifolati 188
zucchini flowers
    Pizza bianca: pumpkin, scamorza and zucchini flowers 136

PIZZA RECIPES

Banana and macadamia sweet calzone 234
Classic calzone 220
Drunken pears, ash-rind goat's cheese 56
Fried pizza margherita 224
Fried pizza with pork belly, ricotta and provola 232
Fried pizza with scarola and crabmeat 228
'Nduja, fior di latte mozzarella, long chillies and goat's cheese 68
Peking duck roll 222
Pizza alla procidana 46
Pizza bianca: beetroot, onion and roast garlic 138
Pizza bianca: black truffle and fontina 148
Pizza bianca: capocollo and fennel 122
Pizza bianca: capocollo, pickled red onion and pecorino 150
Pizza bianca: chickpeas, eggplant and salted ricotta 120
Pizza bianca: chicory, salame and stracciatella 124
Pizza bianca: frutti di mare (seafood) and avocado 118
Pizza bianca: hot calabrese 116
Pizza bianca: lamb belly, ricotta and Mediterranean herbs 146
Pizza bianca: lucariello, onion confettura and burrata 137
Pizza bianca: Montasio, broccoli and prosciutto crackle 132
Pizza bianca: pancetta, wilted rucola and taleggio 126
Pizza bianca: pickled lettuce, capers, olives and tomatoes 152
Pizza bianca: pork and fennel sausage, artichoke, buffalo ricotta 142
Pizza bianca: prawns, zucchini and mint 114
Pizza bianca: prosciutto and bufala 134
Pizza bianca: pumpkin, scamorza and zucchini flowers 136
Pizza bianca: quattro formaggi and walnuts 140
Pizza Capitanata 52

Pizza ricotta, cachi e 'nduja 62
Pizza rossa: calamari, chilli and ginger 108
Pizza rossa: chargrilled vegetables 98
Pizza rossa: Margherita 96
Pizza rossa: marinara Napoletana 94
Pizza rossa: Sicilian capers and anchovies 102
Pizza rossa: tuna, Mediterranean herbs and colatura 106
Rio (Banana and macadamia sweet calzone) 234
Roman pizza filled with cavolo nero frittata and 'nduja 174
Roman pizza margherita 186
Roman pizza with baba ganoush and prawns 190
Roman pizza with broccoli, marinated anchovies and capers 214
Roman pizza with cavolo nero, mushrooms and lardo 194
Roman pizza with crab, broad beans and chilli 210
Roman pizza with cuttlefish, broccoli and chilli 196
Roman pizza with eggplant parmigiana 172
Roman pizza with figs, prosciutto and balsamic 160
Roman pizza with gorgonzola and figs 193
Roman pizza with grilled ox tongue, parsnip purée, salsa verde 166
Roman pizza with lentils, cauliflower and two cheeses 212
Roman pizza with octopus and potato 162
Roman pizza with pork belly, pickled onion and fig jam 176
Roman pizza with potato and braised beef cheeks 202
Roman pizza with potato, calamari, spinach and chilli 206
Roman pizza with prosciutto, burrata and eggplant 158
Roman pizza with red onion 200
Roman pizza with ricotta, persimmons and 'nduja 62
Roman pizza with roast beef, shiitake and grana 192

Roman pizza with roast garlic, tomato and olives 208
Roman pizza with scallops and potato, roast garlic and anchovy dressing 207
Roman pizza with silverbeet, field mushrooms and fontina 178
Roman pizza with tomato and stracciatella 204
Roman pizza with tuna tartare 180
Roman pizza with vitello tonnato 170
Roman pizza with zucchini trifolati 188

OTHER RECIPES

Baba ganoush 190
Banana and macadamia sweet calzone 234
Braised lentils 212
Braised mushrooms 164
Braised peppered beef cheeks 202
Braised silverbeet 178
Broad bean and chilli purée 210
Broccoli cream 132
Caper and olive dressing 162
Cavolo nero frittata 174
Chestnut purée 164
Chickpea purée 120
Confit tomatoes 152
Cooked chicory 124
Fig jam 176
Fried capers 170, 214
Onion confettura 137
Pan-fried broccoli 196
Pan-fried field mushrooms 178
Parsnip purée 166
Pickled lettuce 152
Pickled red onion 150
Prosciutto crackle 132
Pumpkin purée 136
Roast cherry tomatoes 134
Roast duck breast 164
Roast garlic dressing 138
Roast garlic, tomato and olives 208

Roast tomatoes 46
Rosemary oil 130
Salsa verde 166
San Marzano sauce 172
Slow-cooked lamb belly 146
Slow-cooked octopus 162
Slow-cooked onion 52
Slow-roasted pork belly 176
Struffoli 226
Tomato fillets 142
Tuna tartare 180
Vitello tonnato 170
Yellow tomato passata 52

Acknowledgments

There are many pizza-makers that have influenced this book, like Vito Macella at Forno Antico Santa Chiara in Altamura. His durum wheat focaccia sits perfectly with the modern definition of pizza, though it is not in any of the pizza guidebooks. On the other hand, Renato Bosco at Saporè, near Verona, is everywhere that the new movement in pizza is mentioned. His use of diverse grains and natural leavening produce miraculous foundations for his toppings. I have my good friend Paola Calciolari to thank for introducing me to Bosco's pizze some years ago. Though he is often written about as part of the so-called 'gourmet' pizza push, he prefers the term pizza 'contemporanea'. As well I need to mention Massimo Giovannini (Apogeo), Gennaro Battiloro (Kambusa), Stefano Callegari (Sforno), Massimiliano Prete (Gusto Divino), Franco Pepe (Pepe in Grani), Gino Sorbillo (Sorbillo), Antonio Starita (Starita), Giuseppe Concordia (Panificio Adriatico), Vito Zotti (l'Antico Arco) and Daniele Vaccarella (La Braciera).

Thanks to my publisher Sue Hines and the great team at Murdoch Books – Corinne Roberts who steered and kept the book on track, design manager Hugh Ford and the rest of the squad. Thank you Bree Hutchins for the beautiful photography. The Italian leg was a blast watching you devour your first fried pizza in Naples, scoffing a just-made buffalo mozzarella in Paestum and burrata in Andria. Often I would stop the car in the middle of a field of wild fennel, olive trees and trulli in Puglia and off you'd go, camera in hand, on the hunt for the best angle and the best light.

Thank you Frost* for the inspired design of the book. Over the years we've worked on many Manfredi hospitality projects together and it's always a pleasure to work with old friends on new ideas. I'm so glad that Vince Frost and the team could work with us on this project.

Thank you Gianluca Donzelli, extraordinary surfer, chef and pizzaiolo, and my collaborator at Pizzaperta. Thanks to the wonderful team at Pizzaperta – Riccardo, Anya and all the floor staff, and Gianluca, Francesco and the kitchen brigade. Big thanks also to The Star for all your support.

To Antonio Pappalardo, thanks for being my first pizza mentor and a constant companion on many research trips up and down Italy. To Patrick Ricci, thanks for your insightful writings and the many conversations on pizza and its possibilities. To Gabriele Taddeucci, thanks for your support in both Pizzaperta and in this book. To my business partner, Julie Manfredi-Hughes, thank you for your support.

Thanks to the many wonderful artisans, producers and importers that make our pizze delicious and thanks to the visionaries that keep pushing the boundaries of the New Pizza.

Stefano Manfredi

Published in 2017 by Murdoch Books, an imprint of Allen & Unwin
Reprinted 2017
Reprinted 2018

Murdoch Books Australia
83 Alexander Street, Crows Nest NSW 2065
Phone: +61 (0)2 8425 0100
murdochbooks.com.au
info@murdochbooks.com.au

Murdoch Books UK
Ormond House, 26–27 Boswell Street, London WC1N 3JZ
Phone: +44 (0) 20 8785 5995
murdochbooks.co.uk
info@murdochbooks.co.uk

For corporate orders and custom publishing contact our business development team
at salesenquiries@murdochbooks.com.au

Publisher: Corinne Roberts
Design Manager: Hugh Ford
Editorial Manager: Jane Price
Editor: Kay Halsey
Photographer: Bree Hutchins (except pages 20, 22, 23 and 209 Gustarosso Foto;
page 48 Luca Appiotti; page 58 Arianna Giuntini; page 54 and 66 Aromicreativi)
Design Concept: Frost*collective, Sydney
Production Manager: Lou Playfair

ISBN 978 1 74336 881 7 Australia
ISBN 978 1 74336 888 6 UK

A cataloguing-in-publication entry is available from the catalogue of the National Library
of Australia at nla.gov.au
A catalogue record for this book is available from the British Library

Colour reproduction by Splitting Image Colour Studio Pty Ltd, Clayton, Victoria
Printed by C & C Offset Printing, China

MEASURES GUIDE: We have used 20 ml (4 teaspoon) tablespoon measures. If you are
using a 15 ml (3 teaspoon) tablespoon add an extra teaspoon of the ingredient for each
tablespoon specified.